ON THE MANNER OF
NEGOTIATING WITH PRINCES

ON THE MANNER OF NEGOTIATING WITH PRINCES;

on the Uses of Diplomacy ; the Choice of Ministers and Envoys ; and the Personal Qualities necessary for Success in Missions abroad ; by

MONSIEUR DE CALLIÈRES

Councillor-in-Ordinary to the King in Council, Private Secretary to His Majesty, formerly Ambassador Extraordinary and Plenipotentiary of His late Majesty entrusted with the Treaties of Peace concluded at Ryswick, one of the Forty of the French Academy.

Published at Paris by MICHEL BRUNET at the *Mercure Galant*, 1716 ; under Royal Privilege and Approval.

Translated from the French by

A. F. WHYTE

INTRODUCTION

François de Callières' essay on international negotiations is a classic of political literature. His life and writing were concerned with one of the oldest of political processes: transactions between independent political entities called in various historical periods, tribes and clans, peoples and nations, city-states and republics, states and empires. He was Louis XIV's secret agent and later his envoy in several European countries, and represented his sovereign in the negotiations which led to the conclusion of the Treaty of Ryswick in 1697. Subsequently he was secretary to the *Conseil d'État*.

The author was over seventy years old when in 1716 he published his *De la manière de négocier avec les Souverains* and presented it to Philip, Duc d'Orléans, who was Regent of France (1715-1723) after the accession to the throne of the five-year-old Louis XV. Callières wrote his essay in a period of momentous change in Europe and beyond the seas. In the last years of the reign of Louis XIV the War of the Spanish Succession ended with the Treaties of Utrecht (1713) and Rastadt (1714). The unfavorable peace settlement reflected the final failure of Louis XIV's expansionist policy, and the gloomy political atmosphere in France may have stimulated Callières to publication of his reflections on the principles and conditions of successful diplomacy.

ON NEGOTIATING WITH PRINCES

Although diplomacy was more developed in France than in any other European country, in his book Callières complained that good negotiators were rare even there because there were no rules "by which good citizens destined to become negotiators might instruct themselves in the knowledge necessary for this kind of employment." He resented that

> one may see often men who have never left their own country, who have never applied themselves to the study of public affairs, being of meagre intelligence, appointed so to speak over-night to important embassies in countries of which they know neither the interests, the laws, the customs, the language, nor even the geographical situation. And yet I may hazard a guess that there is perhaps no employment in all his Majesty's service more difficult to discharge than that of negotiation. It demands all the penetration, all the dexterity, all the suppleness which a man can well possess. It requires a wide-spread understanding and knowledge, and above all a correct and piercing discernment.

Callières' essay has a more general scope than would appear from the title. His aim was

> to give an idea of the personal qualities and general knowledge necessary in all good negotiators; to indicate to them the paths which they should follow and the rocks which they should avoid; and to exhort those who destine themselves to the foreign service of their country, to render themselves capable of discharging worthily that high, important, and difficult office before entering upon it.

Until recent years the meaning of diplomacy was almost equivalent to negotiation, and so Callières properly discussed negotiation in the broadest sense. This involved the selecting of diplomats, the personal qualities necessary for success in diplomatic missions, and some methods and techniques of diplomacy.

INTRODUCTION

While diplomacy itself is almost as old as recorded history, the techniques of diplomacy and the qualifications of the people involved in a business so removed from the usual experiences of domestic affairs have changed considerably. Since changing social, political and technological conditions have strongly affected the character and functions of diplomacy, it is possible to distinguish diplomacy's permanent features from its transitory elements. Discussion and arrangement of the terms of an agreement between states has been the hub of diplomacy since time immemorial. In this process the human element has remained the constant factor; the political environment and framework, the purpose and methods of negotiations have undergone substantial transformation.

The great empires of Antiquity lived in isolation, and the usual intercourse between them was war. But wars were followed by peace treaties and the conclusion of peace necessitated negotiation. The inviolable character of envoys was recognized even in Antiquity, particularly by the Greek city-states and Rome, although the extent and nature of inviolability changed in the different historical periods. In the close contacts of the Greek city-states, messengers, couriers, heralds, and orators practiced early forms of diplomacy. In the declining period of the Eastern Roman Empire, Byzantine diplomacy endeavored to play neighboring states against each other. For the success of this policy it was necessary to know internal conditions in foreign countries, and so the Byzantine envoy gradually became a professional observer. In addition to negotiating on specific issues he was expected to report on conditions in the foreign countries he visited.

Functional ramifications and the niceties of diplomacy were further developed by the Papal Court of Rome and particularly by Venice and other city-states in Northern Italy from the thirteenth century onward. Until the French invasion in 1494 the north Italian cities were somewhat removed from the rivalries of the major territorial monarchies of Europe and could engage in competition among themselves. Their international practice was comparable to the modern system of national states which has characterized European politics for the last four centuries. In the second half of the fifteenth century the northern Italian city-states began to establish permanent diplomatic missions, a practice soon followed by European monarchies. Until that time ambassadors were sent on special occasions only and their missions were of temporary character.

After the breakdown of the medieval order and the emergence of the national state as a basic unit in international relations, the peace of Europe was secured by the balance of power. Roughly until the French Revolution and Napoleonic wars, a multiple balance prevailed in Europe most of the time. Although the separate balances interacted on some occasions, they facilitated independent developments in various regions of the Continent. This new system made possible many political combinations, flexible policies, and changes in alliances, and thus required frequent negotiation between rulers. Because of this new political situation and the increasing trade relations, diplomacy became more important and was approaching what was to be its golden age in the seventeenth century. As Callières explained:

> To understand the permanent use of diplomacy and the necessity for continual negotiations, we must think of the states of which Europe is composed as being joined together by all kinds of necessary commerce, in such a way that they may be regarded as members of one Republic and that no considerable change can take place in any one of them without affecting the condition, or dis-

turbing the peace, of all the others. The blunder of the smallest of sovereigns may indeed cast an apple of discord among all the greatest Powers, because there is no state so great which does not find it useful to have relations with the lesser states and to seek friends among the different parties of which even the smallest state is composed. History teems with the results of these conflicts which often have their beginnings in small events, easy to control or suppress at their birth, but which when grown in magnitude became the causes of long and bloody wars which have ravaged the principal states of Christendom.

The growth of diplomacy in France was facilitated by a centralized government and a professional non-feudal administration. Cardinal Richelieu concentrated the responsibility for all aspects of foreign affairs in the Foreign Ministry (1626), and in his famous *Testament Politique* he put forward diplomatic principles of permanent value. Callières considered Richelieu as the model for all statesmen, "to whom France owes a very great debt."

If after Richelieu's time French diplomacy became a model in many ways for European states, the selection of diplomats and the method of negotiations still did not follow generally accepted patterns. Callières apparently had some untoward experiences during his diplomatic career, and probably considered it his civic duty to call attention to the importance of diplomatic negotiations and to examine in detail the qualities of a good negotiator. He suggests that the qualities necessary for success are "an observant mind, a spirit of application which refuses to be distracted by pleasures or frivolous amusements, a sound judgment which takes the measure of things as they are, and which goes straight to its goal by the shortest and most natural paths without wandering into useless refinements and subtleties which as a rule only succeed in repelling those with whom one is dealing." Callières particularly warns against the air of mystery, "in which secrets are made out of nothing and in which the merest bagatelle is exalted into a great matter of state. . . ." This mark of smallness of mind "betokens an incapacity to take the true measure either of men or of things." An ambassador must show that the "ordinary sentiments of the human heart move in him, for there is no kind of employment in which at the same time elevation and nobility of spirit and a kindly courtesy in little things are more necessary." He warns against the air of superiority. A good negotiator must be free from "wayward humours and fantasies" and he must know "how to suffer fools gladly, how to accommodate himself to the changing humours of others." Since the ambassador himself paid the expenses of his office, wealth was important. A wise prince, however, "will serve his own interests much better by choosing an able negotiator of mediocre fortune than one endowed with all the wealth of the Indies but possessing a small intelligence, for it is obvious that the rich man may not know the true use of riches, whereas the able man will assuredly know how to employ his own ability."

Callières was convinced that diplomacy was a profession by itself, which necessitated apprenticeship and the same preparations and assiduity of attention that men gave to other recognized professions such as a military career. He considered it folly "to entrust the conduct of negotiations to an untrained amateur unless he has conspicuously shown in some other walk of life the qualities and knowledge necessary for the practice of diplomacy." In view of the importance of the proper representation of state interests abroad,

> both the prince himself and his ministers must steel
> themselves to resist the pressure of friends and relations

who seek employment for unworthy persons. In diplomacy . . . the best minds, the most sagacious and instructed of public servants should be appointed to the principal foreign posts regardless of the personal affairs of the prince himself or the party attachments of the chosen ambassadors.

Callières thought that diplomatic gifts were unusual, and, therefore, that diplomatic genius was born and not made. He added that genius is not a substitute for good manners, and he stressed that many qualities may be developed by practice and that knowledge can be acquired by study. Moreover, he considered it necessary that a diplomat should have the capacity to profit by travel and that he should know German, Italian, Spanish, and Latin. Since French had become the *lingua franca* of diplomacy during the seventeenth and eighteenth centuries, and since even the Holy Roman Empire of the German Nation was willing to conclude the Treaty of Rastadt in French, his emphasis on the importance of foreign language is remarkable. His work abounds in observations, which in the manner of classics have present-day relevance. In connection with science he gave an advice valid even today:

It is also very useful and fitting for the diplomat . . . to have such a general knowledge of science as may tend to the development of his understanding, but he must be master of his scientific knowledge and not be consumed by it.

In negotiations themselves, Callières emphasized the importance of the adaptability of diplomats to a foreign environment and proposed drastic measures against incompetent men.

It is a crime against the public safety not to uproot incapacity wherever it is discovered, or to allow an incompetent diplomatist to remain one moment longer than necessary in a place where competency is sorely needed.

Callières repeatedly emphasized the necessity of honesty, good faith, and firmness. He warned the negotiator against appearing to be a skilled manipulator:

> . . . the negotiator must appear as an agreeable, enlightened, and far-seeing person; he must beware of trying to pass himself off too conspicuously as a crafty or adroit manipulator. The essence of skill lies in concealing it, and the negotiator must ever strive to leave an impression upon his fellow diplomatists of his sincerity and good faith.

His emphasis on good faith, honesty, and the necessity of the creation of an atmosphere of mutual confidence in negotiations is of considerable importance because the popular mind has been inclined to identify diplomacy with falsehood and lies. Deceit was not objectionable in the early stages of diplomacy in the Greek city-states, and in the Byzantine Empire it became an art. Diplomacy among the Italian city-states permitted practically all means for promotion of the objectives of the state. Sir Henry Wotton inscribed in the album of a friend in Augsburg that *Legatus est vir bonus peregre missus ad mentiendum Reipublicae causa* ("An ambassador is an honest man, sent to lie abroad for the good of his country"). Although this comment was made in jest in 1604 and most English translations exaggerated its original meaning, it contributed to the strengthening of a widely accepted false idea about diplomacy. Callières denied energetically that lies are necessary in negotiations and suggested time and again that honesty is the best policy. He discussed many other personal qualities of good negotiators, and other conditions necessary for diplomatic success. He recommended that in countries such as England and Poland, where the Parliament or Diet shared national sovereignty with the prince, the good negotiator should know where to find the balance of domestic power. He did not fail to point out the importance of spies, and spoke with admiration of the Spanish Court which provided the Spanish ambassadors with secret funds. In Callières' time the European system differed greatly from contemporary conditions. The interdependence of the world to-day is greater than it was among the states of Europe in the eighteenth century. In our expanding state system, diplomatic methods and procedures have greatly diversified. Socially imaginative minds in diplomacy are much more important today than in bygone times. As a result of revolutions in the fields of transportation and communication, the ability of governments to receive information of world events and to send instructions quickly to their diplomatic representatives has greatly influenced relations between envoys and governments. Almost instantaneous communication has facilitated control by the government of its representatives abroad. In turn, the envoys can more easily influence policy of their governments through the same communications. In recent decades international agencies have become new theaters for diplomatic activity; open diplomacy by conference, introduced by the League of Nations and further developed by the United Nations, has changed many aspects of diplomacy. Diplomacy has broadened and its methods embrace new fields.

Although the various old and new forms of diplomacy necessarily operate within the power realities of a divided and greatly diversified world, some basic human conditions have not changed in international politics, and Callières was a connoisseur of this constant element in diplomacy. Since human nature remains the same, most of Callières' comments and maxims have lasting value. His observations could have been addressed to the White House, Capitol Hill, and the

Department of State. His essay has long been considered a rich source for basic problems of diplomacy and useful reading for all students of foreign affairs. Sir Ernest Satow called it "a mine of political wisdom," and Sir Harold Nicolson noted in his study on *The Evolution of Diplomacy* that Callières' book "remains to this day the best manual of diplomatic method ever written."

Stephen D. Kertesz
September 27, 1963
Notre Dame, Indiana

ON THE MANNER OF
NEGOTIATING WITH PRINCES

To His Royal Highness, Monseigneur le
Duc d'Orléans, Regent of the Kingdom.

MONSEIGNEUR,—This work, which I have the honour to present to your Royal Highness, has for its aim : to give an idea of the personal qualities and general knowledge necessary in all good negotiators ; to indicate to them the paths which they should follow and the rocks which they should avoid ; and to exhort those who destine themselves to the foreign service of their country, to render themselves capable of discharging worthily that high, important, and difficult office before entering upon it.

The honour which the late King did me in charging me with his commands and his full powers for foreign negotiation, and particularly for those which led to the Treaty of Ryswick, has redoubled the attention which I have ever paid since my youngest years to my own instruction in the power, the rights, and the ambitions of each of the principal monarchies and states of Europe, in their divergent interests and the forms of their government, in the causes of their understandings and misunder-

3

standings, and finally in the treaties which they have made one with another ; in order to employ this knowledge to the best advantage whenever occasion offered in the service of my King and Country. After the loss which France has just suffered of that great King, whose reign was so full of glory and triumph, she did indeed need that the Hand of God, which has always upheld her in her necessities, should continue to guide her. We had indeed to look for Divine Help to support us during the minority of his present Majesty, so that we might hope that the All-Powerful Hand should mould a prince of like blood and spirit to him who has gone. The Regency needed an intelligence of the highest order, a capacity without limit, a clear insight into the character of persons and events, and an indefatigable activity which would increase at every new demand made by the interests of state —all these united in the person of a prince at once just, lovable, beneficent, whose character might earn for him the title of a veritable father of his country. These are the traits so strongly and so profoundly marked in you, Monseigneur, which have brought all France on its knees in homage before you, with full confidence and happiness, and a glorious prestige which shall pass undimmed to our remotest descendants as a worthy symbol of your great rule.

NEGOTIATING WITH PRINCES

I am, with profound respect, and with a zealous and affectionate attachment to your Person, Monseigneur,

Your Royal Highness's most humble, obedient, and faithful servant,

De CALLIERES.

THE art of negotiation with princes is so important that the fate of the greatest states often depends upon the good or bad conduct of negotiations and upon the degree of capacity in the negotiators employed. Thus monarchs and their ministers of state cannot examine with too great care the natural or acquired qualities of those citizens whom they despatch on missions to foreign states to entertain there good relations with their masters, to make treaties of peace, of alliance, of commerce or of other kinds, or to hinder other Powers from concluding such treaties to the prejudice of their own master ; and generally, to take charge of those interests which may be affected by the diverse conjunctures of events. Every Christian prince must take as his chief maxim not to employ arms to support or vindicate his rights until he has employed and exhausted the way of reason and of persuasion. It is to his interest also, to add to reason and persuasion the influence of benefits conferred, which indeed is one of the surest ways to make his own power secure, and to increase it. But above all he must employ good labourers in his service, such indeed as know how to employ all these methods for the best, and how to gain the hearts and wills of men, for it is in this that the science of negotiation principally consists.

French Neglect of Diplomacy. Our nation is so warlike that we can hardly conceive of any other kind of glory or of honour than those won in the profession of arms. Hence it is that the greater number of Frenchmen of good birth apply themselves with zeal to the profession of arms in order that they may gain advancement therein, but they neglect the study of the various interests which divide Europe and which are a source of frequent wars. This inclination and natural application in our people result in a rich supply of good general officers, and we need have no surprise that it is considered that no gentleman of quality can receive a high command in the armies of the King who has not already passed through all these stages by which a soldier may equip himself for war.

But, alas, it is not the same with our negotiators. They are indeed rare among us because there has been in general no discipline nor fixed rules of the foreign service of his Majesty by which good citizens destined to become negotiators might instruct themselves in the knowledge necessary for this kind of employment. And indeed we find that instead of gradual promotion by degrees and by the evidence of proved capacity and experience, as is the case in the usages of war, one may see often men who have never left their own country, who have never applied themselves to the study of public affairs, being of meagre intelligence, appointed so to speak over-night to important embassies in countries of which they know neither the interests, the laws, the customs, the language, nor even the geographical situation. And yet I may hazard a guess that there is perhaps no employment in all his Majesty's service more difficult to discharge than that of negotiation. It demands all the penetration, all the dexterity, all the suppleness which a man can well possess. It requires a widespread understanding and knowledge, and above all a correct and piercing discernment.

It causes me no surprise that men who have embarked on this career for the sake of titles and emoluments, having not the least idea of the real duties of their post, have occasioned grave harm to the public interest during their apprenticeship to this service. These novices in negotiation become easily intoxicated with honours done in their person to the dignity of their royal master. They are like the ass in the fable who received for himself all the incense burned before the statue of the goddess which he bore on his back. This happens

Diplomacy an Expert Craft.

9

above all to those who are employed by a great monarch on missions to princes of a lower order, for they are apt to place in their addresses the most odious comparisons, as well as veiled threats, which are really only a mark of weakness. Such ambassadors do not fail to bring upon themselves the aversion of the court to which they are accredited, and they resemble heralds of arms rather than ambassadors whose principal aim is ever to maintain a good correspondence between their master and the princes to whom they are accredited. In all cases they should represent the power of their own sovereign as a means of maintaining and increasing that of the foreign court, instead of using it as an odious comparison designed to humiliate and contemn. These misfortunes and many others, which are the result of the lack of capacity and of the foolish conduct of many citizens employed by princes to deal with public affairs abroad, occasioned in me the belief that it is by no means impertinent to set down some observations on the manner of negotiating with sovereigns and with their ministers, on the qualities necessary for those who mean to adopt the profession of diplomacy, and on the means which wise princes will take to secure a good choice of men well adapted at once to the profession of negotiation and to the different countries where they may be sent. But before I take my subject in detail it is perhaps well that I should explain the use and the necessity for princes to maintain continual negotiation in the form of permanent embassies to all great states, both in neighbouring countries and in those more distant, in war as well as in peace.

To understand the permanent use of diplomacy and the necessity for continual negotiations, we *The Usefulness of Negotiation.* must think of the states of which Europe is composed as being joined together by all kinds of necessary commerce, in such a way that they may be regarded as members of one Republic and that no considerable change can take place in any one of them without affecting the condition, or disturbing the peace, of all the others. The blunder of the smallest of sovereigns may indeed cast an apple of discord among all the greatest Powers, because there is no state so great which does not find it useful to have relations with the lesser states and to seek friends among the different parties of which even the smallest state is composed. History teems with the results of these conflicts which often have their beginnings in small events, easy to control or suppress at their birth, but which when grown in magnitude became the causes of long and bloody wars which have ravaged the principal states of Christendom. Now these actions and reactions between one state and another oblige the sagacious monarch and his ministers to maintain a continual process of diplomacy in all such states for the purpose of recording events as they occur and of reading their true meaning with diligence and exactitude. One may say that knowledge of this kind is one of the most important and necessary features of good government, because indeed the domestic peace of the state depends largely upon appropriate measures taken in its foreign service to make friends among well-disposed states, and by timely action to resist those who cherish hostile designs. There is indeed no prince so powerful that he can afford to neglect the assistance offered by a good alliance, in resisting the forces of hostile powers which are prompted by jealousy of his property to unite in a hostile coalition.

The Diplomat: An Agent of High Policy. Now, the enlightened and assiduous negotiator serves not only to discover all projects and cabals by which coalitions may arise against his prince in the country where he is sent to negotiate, but also to dissipate their very beginnings by giving timely advice. It is easy to destroy even the greatest enterprises at their birth ; and as they often require several springs to give them motion, it can hardly be possible for a hostile intrigue to ripen without knowledge of it coming to the ears of an attentive negotiator living in the place where it is being hatched. The able negotiator will know how to profit by the various dispositions and changes which arise in the country where he lives, not merely in order to frustrate designs hostile to the interests of his master, but also for the positive and fruitful purpose of bringing to an apt result those other designs which may work to his advantage. By his industry and application he may himself produce changes of opinion favourable to the office which he has to discharge ; indeed, if he do but once in an apt moment catch the tide at the flood he may confer a benefit on his prince a hundredfold greater than any expense in treasure or personal effort which he may have put forth. Now if a monarch should wait, before sending his envoys to countries near and far, until important events occur—as for instance, until it is a question of hindering the conclusion of some treaty which confers advantage on an enemy Power, or a declaration of war against an ally which would deprive the monarch himself of the assistance of that very ally for other purposes —it will be found that the negotiators, sent thus at the eleventh hour on urgent occasions, have no time to explore the terrain or to study the habits of mind of the foreign court or to create the necessary liaisons or to change the course of events already in full flood, unless indeed they bring with them enormous sums whose disbursement must weigh heavily on the treasury of their master, and which run the risk, in truth, of being paid too late.

Cardinal Richelieu, whom I set before me as the model for all statesmen, to whom France owes a very great debt, maintained a system of unbroken diplomacy in all manner of countries, and beyond question he thus drew enormous advantage for his master. He bears witness to this truth in his own political testament, speaking thus :—

'The states of Europe enjoy all the advantages of continual negotiation in the measure in which they are conducted with prudence. No one could believe how great these advantages are who has not had experience of them. I confess that it was not till I had had five or six years' experience of the management of high affairs that I realised this truth, but I am now so firmly persuaded of it that I will boldly say that the service which a regular and unbroken system of diplomacy, conducted both in public and in secret in all countries, even where no immediate fruit can be gathered, is one of the first necessities for the health and welfare of the state. I can say with truth that in my time I have seen the face of affairs in France and in Christendom completely changed because under the authority of his Majesty I have been enabled to practise this principle which till my time had been absolutely neglected by the ministers of this kingdom.' The Cardinal says further : ' The light of nature teaches each of us in his private life to maintain relations with his neighbours because as their near presence enables them to injure so it also enables them to do us service, just as the surroundings of a city either hinder or facilitate the approach to it.' And he adds : ' The meaner sort of men confine their outlook within the cities where they were born. But those to whom God has given a greater light will neglect no means of improvement whether it come from near or from far.' The evidence of this great genius demands all the greater consideration because the high services which he rendered to his King by means of negotiation convincingly prove that he speaks the truth. No considerable event occurred in Europe during his ministry in which he did not play a great part, and he was often the principal agent in the great movements of his time. He it was who designed the revolution in Portugal in 1640, by which the legitimate heir to the Crown resumed the throne. He profited by the discontent of the Catalans who rose in revolt in that same year. He did not hesitate to encourage negotiations even with the African Moors. Previously he brought his labours to success in the north by persuading Gustavus Adolphus, King of Sweden, to invade Germany, and thus to deliver her from slavery to the House of

Austria which then reigned despotically, dethroning her princes and disposing of their states and their titles to its own court minions. Rumour even attributes the revolution in Bohemia to the action of Cardinal Richelieu. He formed and maintained several leagues ; he won for France many great allies who contributed to the success of his high designs, in which the abasement of the prodigious power of the House of Austria was always the chief ; and throughout all these designs we can trace the unbroken thread of a well-maintained system of diplomacy, acting as the obedient and capable agent of the great minister himself, whose profound capacity and vast genius thus found a favourable field of action.

Value of Diplomacy. It is not necessary to turn far back into the past in order to understand what can be achieved by negotiation. We see daily around us its definite effects in sudden revolutions favourable to this great design of state or that, in the use of sedition in fermenting the hatreds between nations, in causing jealous rivals to arm against one another so that the *tertius gaudens* may profit, in the formation of leagues and other treaties of various kinds between monarchs whose interests might otherwise clash, in the dissolution by crafty means of the closest unions between states : in a word, one may say that the art of negotiation, according as its conduct is good or evil, gives form to great affairs and may turn a host of lesser events into a useful influence upon the course of the greater. Indeed, we can see in diplomacy thus conducted a greater influence in many ways upon the conduct and fortunes of mankind than even in the laws which they themselves have designed, for the reason that, however scrupulous private man may be in obedience to the law, misunderstandings and conflicts of ambition easily arise between nations, and cannot be settled by a process of law but only by a convention between the contending parties. It is on the occasion of such conventions that diplomacy plays a decisive part.

It is thus easy to conclude that a small number of well-chosen negotiators posted in the different states in Europe may render to their sovereign and their state the greatest services ; that a single word or act may do more than the invasion of whole armies because the crafty negotiator will know how to set in motion various forces native to the country in which he is negotiating, and thus may spare his master the vast expense of a campaign. Nothing can be more useful than a timely diversion thus set on foot.

It is also of high interest to all great princes that their negotiators should be of such character and standing as to act appropriately as mediators in the disputes between other sovereigns and to produce peace by the authority of their intervention. Nothing can contribute more to the reputation, the power, and the universal respect of a monarch, than to be served by those who themselves inspire respect and confidence. A powerful prince who maintains a constant system of diplomacy served by wise and instructed negotiators in the different states of Europe, and who thus cultivates well-chosen friendships and maintains useful sources of information, is in a position to influence the destiny of neighbouring foreign states, to maintain peace between all states, or to pursue war where it is favourable to his design. In all these concerns the prosperity of his plans and the greatness of his name depend first and last on the conduct and qualities of the negotiators to whom he entrusts his services. So now we examine in detail the qualities necessary for a good negotiator.

Personal Qualities of the Good Negotiator. God having endowed men with diverse talents, the best advice that one can give is to take counsel with themselves before choosing their profession. Thus he who would enter the profession of diplomacy must examine himself to see whether he was born with the qualities necessary for success. These qualities are an observant mind, a spirit of application which refuses to be distracted by pleasures or frivolous amusements, a sound judgment which takes the measure of things as they are, and which goes straight to its goal by the shortest and most natural paths without wandering into useless refinements and subtleties which as a rule only succeed in repelling those with whom one is dealing. The negotiator must further possess that penetration which enables him to discover the thoughts of men and to know by the least movement of their countenances what passions are stirring within, for such movements are often betrayed even by the most practised negotiator. He must also have a mind so fertile in expedients as easily to smooth away the difficulties which he meets in the course of his duty ; he must have presence of mind to find a quick and pregnant reply even to unforeseen surprises, and by such judicious replies he must be able to recover himself when his foot has slipped. An equable humour, a tranquil and patient nature, always ready to listen with attention to those whom he meets ; an address always open, genial, civil, agreeable, with easy and ingratiating manners which assist largely in making a favourable impression upon those around him— these things are the indispensable adjuncts to the negotiator's profession. Their opposite, the grave and cold air, a melancholy or rough exterior, may create a first impression which is not easily removed. Above all the good negotiator must have sufficient control over himself to resist the longing to speak before he has really thought what he shall say. He should not endeavour to gain the reputation of being able to reply immediately and without premeditation to every proposition which is made, and he should take a special care not to fall into the error of one famous foreign ambassador of our time who so loved an argument that each time he warmed up in controversy he revealed important secrets in order to support his opinion.

The Air of Mystery.

But indeed there is another fault of which the negotiator must beware : he must not fall into the error of supposing that an air of mystery, in which secrets are made out of nothing and in which the merest bagatelle is exalted into a great matter of state, is anything but a mark of smallness of mind and betokens an incapacity to take the true measure either of men or of things. Indeed, the more the negotiator clothes himself in mystery, the less he will have means of discovering what is happening and of acquiring the confidence of those with whom he deals. A continual reserve is like the lock on a door which is never turned and becomes so rusty that in the end no man can open it. The able negotiator will of course not permit his secret to be drawn from him except at his own time, and he should be able to disguise from his competitor the fact that he has any secret to reveal ;

20

but in all other matters he must remember that
open dealing is the foundation of confidence and
that everything which he is not compelled by duty
to withhold ought to be freely shared with those
around him. He will thus gradually establish
terms of confidence with his neighbours, from
which he may draw immense profit, for it may not
infrequently happen that in exchange for some
trivial information given by himself, the negotiator
may, as it were by accident, receive important news
from his colleague in another embassy. The
practised negotiator will know how to employ the
circumstances of his life and of the lives of those
around him in such a manner as to lead them naturally and without restraint to talk of the conditions
and affairs of their own country, and the more extended his view and the wider his knowledge the
more surely will he thus gather important news
every day of his life.

Let it not be supposed, however, that the good *Dignity.*
negotiator requires only the light of a high intellect,
dexterity, and other fine qualities of the mind.
He must show that the ordinary sentiments of the
human heart move in him, for there is no kind of
employment in which at the same time elevation
and nobility of spirit and a kindly courtesy in little
things are more necessary. An ambassador indeed
resembles in a certain sense the actor placed before

the eyes of the public in order that he may play a great part, for his profession raises him above the ordinary condition of mankind and makes him in some sort the equal of the masters of the earth by that right of representation which attaches to his service, and by the special relations which his office gives him with the mighty ones of the earth. He must therefore be able to simulate a dignity even if he possess it not ; but this obligation is the rock upon which many an astute negotiator has perished because he did not know in what dignity consisted. No negotiation was ever assisted by open or veiled menaces merely for their own sake, and negotiators too often confuse a proud and arrogant bearing with that careful dignity which ought to clothe their office. To advance pretensions or to demand excessive privileges is merely the sign of pride and of a desire to extract from the privileged position of an ambassador a personal and unworthy advantage, in the doing of which an ambitious negotiator may easily and utterly compromise the whole authority of his master. No man who enters diplomacy in a spirit of avarice or with a desire to seek interests other than those of his service, or merely with the desire to earn the applause of the crowd, or to attract esteem and recompense from his master, will ever make success in negotiation. And even if some important duty may be well dis-

charged in his hands, it is only to be attributed
to some happy conjuncture of events which in itself
smoothed away all difficulties.

To maintain the dignity of diplomacy the ne- *Influence of*
gotiator must clothe himself in liberality and *Women.*
generosity of heart, even in magnificence, but all
with care and a frugality of design so that the trap-
pings of his office do not by their display outshine
the sterling merits of his own character and person.
Let clean linen and appointments and delicacy
reign at his table. Let him frequently give ban-
quets and diversions in honour of the principal
persons of the court in which he lives, and even
in the honour of the prince himself, if he so cares
to take part. Let him also enter into the spirit
of the same diversions offered by others, but always
in a light, unconstrained, and agreeable manner,
and always with an open, good-natured, straightforward air, and with a continual desire to give
pleasure to others. If the custom of the country
in which he serves permits freedom of conversation
with the ladies of the court, he must on no account
neglect any opportunity of placing himself and his
master in a favourable light in the eyes of these
ladies, for it is well known that the power of feminine
charm often extends to cover the weightiest reso-
lutions of state. The greatest events have sometimes followed the toss of a fan or the nod of a head.

ON THE MANNER OF

But let him beware ! Let him do all things in his power, by the magnificence of his display, by the polish, attraction, and gallantry of his person, to engage their pleasure, but let him beware lest he engage his own heart. He must never forget that Love's companions are Indiscretion and Imprudence, and that the moment he becomes pledged to the whim of a favoured woman, no matter how wise he may be, he runs a grave risk of being no longer master of his own secrets. We have often seen terrible results follow from this kind of weakness into which even the greatest ministers are liable to fall, and we need go no further than our own time for remarkable examples and warnings.

Power of the Purse. Now, as the surest way of gaining the good-will of a prince is to gain the good graces of those who have most influence upon his mind, a good negotiator must reinforce his own good manners, his insight of character, and attraction of person by certain expenses which will largely assist in opening his road before him. But these expenses must be laid out in the proper measure. They must be made by a careful design ; and wherever large gifts are offered, the giver must take care beforehand to know that they will be received in the right spirit and above all that they will not be refused. I do not mean that there are not countries where no great art is needed in the matter of giving gifts.

NEGOTIATING WITH PRINCES

In such a country they are no longer gifts but bribes; but it is always to be remembered that there is a certain delicacy to be observed in all commerce of this kind, and that a gift presented in the right spirit, at the right moment, by the right person, may act with tenfold power upon him who receives it. There are various established customs in different countries by which occasion arises for making small presents. This kind of expense, though it occasions but a small outlay of money, may contribute largely to the esteem in which an ambassador is held and acquire for him friends at the court to which he is accredited. And, indeed, the manner in which this little custom is carried out may have an important bearing upon high policy. And, of course, in such a matter the practised negotiator will soon be aware that at every court there are certain persons of greater wit than fortune who will not refuse a small gratification or secret subsidy which may bring in large results, for the wit of these persons enables them to maintain a confidential position at court without that personal splendour which the rich nobleman can display. Such persons I say may be of great use to the clever negotiator. Among amusements, for instance, the dancers, who by the fact of their profession have an *entrée* less formal and in some degree more intimate with the prince than any ambassador can perhaps possess, are often to be found valuable agents in negotiation. Or again, it happens that a monarch has around him certain officers of low rank entrusted with duties which bring them in close contact both with their master and with his minister's mind, and a timely present aptly given may reveal important secrets. And finally, even great ministers of state themselves may not be inaccessible by the same means.

Secret Service. It frequently happens in negotiation as in war that well-chosen spies contribute more than any other agency to the success of great plans, and indeed it is clear that there is nothing so well adapted to upset the best design as the sudden and premature revelation of an important secret upon which it depends. And as there is no expense better designed nor more necessary than that which is laid out upon a secret service, it would be inexcusable for a minister of state to neglect it. The general will say with truth that he would sooner have one regiment the less than a poorly equipped system of espionage, and that he would perhaps even forgo reinforcements if he could be accurately informed of the disposition and numbers of the enemy armies. Similarly let an ambassador retrench all superfluous expense in order that he may have the funds at his disposal to maintain a secret service which will inform him of all that happens in the foreign country of his service. Yet despite the universal acknowledged truth of what I say, most negotiators will more readily spend vast sums on a great show of horses and carriages, on rows of useless flunkeys, than on the payment of a few well-chosen agents who could keep them supplied with news. In this matter we should learn a lesson from the Spaniards, who never neglect their secret agents—a fact which I am sure has contributed largely to the success of their ministers in many important negotiations. It is doubtless the success of Spanish agents which has led to the establishment of the wise custom of the Spanish Court to give Spanish ambassadors an extraordinary fund called *Gastos Secretos.*

The ambassador has sometimes been called an honourable spy because one of his principal occupations is to discover great secrets; and he fails in the discharge of his duty if he does not know how to lay out the necessary sums for this purpose. Therefore an ambassador should be a man born with a liberal hand ready to undertake willingly large expenses of this kind; and he must be even prepared to do it at his own charges when the emoluments of his master are insufficient. For as his principal aim must be to succeed, that interest should eclipse all others in any man truly devoted to

The Honourable Spy.

his profession and capable of succeeding in it. But, on the other hand, the sagacious prince will not neglect the equipment of his negotiators with every possible means for acquiring friends and secret agents in all countries where his interests are at stake, for these expenses well laid out bring back a large return with usury to the prince who makes them, and do much to smooth away the difficulties which lie in the path of his designs. And he will soon be aware that if he does not employ this expedient his ministers can indeed make but little progress in their negotiations. He will win no new allies but risk losing old ones.

Courage. Courage is a most necessary quality in a negotiator ; for, though the law of nations should give him ample security, there are many occasions in which he will find himself in danger, where he will have to rely upon his own courage and resource to escape from a perilous position without compromising the negotiation on which he is engaged. Thus no timid man can hope to conduct secret designs to success : unforeseen accidents will shake his faith, and in a moment of fear he may too easily give away his secrets even by the passing expression of his countenance and by the manner of his speech. And indeed a too great concern for his personal safety may lead him to take measures highly prejudicial to the duties he has to discharge. And at

times when the honour of his master is attacked
his timidity may prevent him from maintaining
with the necessary vigour the dignity of his office
and the prestige of his King. A prelate who was
an ambassador at Rome from King Francis I.
brought disgrace on his master because he failed
to defend him in the Consistory, where the Emperor,
Charles V., attempted to cast upon the French
King the whole responsibility for the continuation
of the war, boasting falsely that he had offered to
end it by a single combat with François himself,
and that the French King had refused. The King
was so furious that he gave the Emperor the lie in
public, and made known to the world his displeasure
with his own ambassador for failing to uphold the
dignity of France. François there and then took
the resolution never to employ any man as French
ambassador who was not a practised swordsman,
and thus he hoped to uphold the honour of his
house.

A good negotiator must not only be courageous *Firmness in*
in danger but firm in debate. There are many *Dispute.*
men who are naturally brave, but cannot maintain
an opinion in dispute. The kind of firmness that
is needed is that which, having carefully and fully
examined the matter, consents to no compromise
but pursues with constancy a resolution once
adopted till it is carried into effect. Compromise

is the easy refuge of the irresolute spirit. The lack of firmness of which I speak here is a common fault of those who have a lively imagination .for every kind of accident which may befall, and hinders them from determining with vigour and despatch the means by which action should be taken. They will look at a matter on so many sides that they forget in which direction they are travelling. This irresolution is most prejudicial to the conduct of great affairs which demand a decisive spirit, acting upon a careful balance of advantage and disadvantage, and pursuing the main purpose without abatement. It is said that Cardinal Richelieu, who perhaps took wider views than any man of his time, was somewhat irresolute when he came to action, and that Father Joseph, the Capuchin, a much narrower intelligence than the Cardinal, was of the greatest value to him because, once a decision was taken, he pursued it tenaciously, and often assisted the Cardinal in dismissing designs of compromise by which crafty persons hoped to destroy the original plan.

Genius no Substitute for Good Manners. There are some geniuses born with such an elevation of character and superiority of mind that they have a natural ascendancy over all whom they meet. But a negotiator of this kind must take good care not to rely too much on his own judgment in order to voice that superiority which

30

he has over other men, for it may earn for him a reputation for arrogance and hardness; and just on account of his very elevation above the level of common humanity, events may escape him, and he may be the dupe of his own self-confidence. He must sometimes consent to meet smaller men on their own ground.

The good negotiator, moreover, will never found *Value of Good* the success of his mission on promises which he *Faith.* cannot redeem or on bad faith. It is a capital error, which prevails widely, that a clever negotiator must be a master of the art of deceit. Deceit indeed is but a measure of the smallness of mind of him who employs it, and simply shows that his intelligence is too meagrely equipped to enable him to arrive at his ends by just and reasonable methods. No doubt the art of lying has been practised with success in diplomacy; but unlike that honesty which here as elsewhere is the best policy, a lie always leaves a drop of poison behind, and even the most dazzling diplomatic success gained by dishonesty stands on an insecure foundation, for it awakes in the defeated party a sense of aggravation, a desire for vengeance, and a hatred which must always be a menace to his foe. Even if deceit were not as despicable to every right-minded man as it is, the negotiator will perhaps bear in mind that he will be engaged throughout life upon the affairs of

31

diplomacy, and that it is therefore his interest to establish a reputation for plain and fair dealing so that men may know that they can rely upon him ; for one negotiation successfully carried through by the honesty and high intelligence of a diplomatist will give him a great advantage in other enterprises on which he embarks in the future. In every country where he goes he will be received with esteem and pleasure, and men will say of him and of his master that their cause is too good to be served by evil means. For if the negotiator is obliged to observe with faithfulness all the promises which he has made, it will be at once seen that both he himself and the prince whom he serves are to be relied on.

Perils of Deceit.

This is surely a well-known truth and so indispensable a duty that it would appear superfluous to recommend it. At the same time many negotiators have been so corrupted by converse usages that they have forgotten the uses of truth—upon which I shall make but one observation, which is, that the prince or minister who has been deceived by his own negotiator probably began by teaching that negotiator the lesson of deception ; or, if he did not, he suffers because he has made the choice of a bad servant. It is not enough to choose a clever and well-instructed man for the discharge of high political duties. The agent in such affairs

32

must be a man of probity and one who loves truth, for otherwise there can be no confidence in him. It is true that this probity is not often found joined to that capacity for taking wide views which is so necessary to a diplomatist, nor is it always found in a man well stored with all the necessary knowledge which we have already described as the equipment of a good negotiator. I may be reminded that a prince is often obliged to use diverse instruments in order to accomplish his ends, and that there have been men of little virtue who proved themselves great negotiators and in whose hands high affairs of state have prospered, and that men of this type being restrained by no scruples have more often succeeded in delicate negotiations than have the right men who have employed none but honest means.

But let it be remarked that the prince who entrusts his negotiations to this type of diplomatist cannot count upon their good services except as long as he himself is prosperous. In difficult times, or at moments when disgrace seems to have fallen upon him, these master-rogues will be the first to betray him and to take service on the side of the strong. Here then we find the final recommendation of the necessity of employing honest men. I am reminded of the fine reply of Monsieur de Faber, who was Marshal of France, to Cardinal

Monsieur de Faber rebukes Cardinal Mazarin.

33

Mazarin when this great minister wished to bring over a man of substance, who shall be nameless, to his own party. He entrusted the delicate duty to Monsieur de Faber, charging him to offer great promises which he admitted he was not in a position to redeem. Monsieur de Faber refused the commission in these words : ' Monseigneur, you will find many men ready to carry false messages ; but you have some need of 'honest men to speak the truth. I beg of you to retain me for the latter service.'

Loose Livers make Bad Negotiators. Finally, it is in a high degree dangerous to entrust an important negotiation to a man of irregular life whose domestic and personal habits are disorderly. How can one expect of such a man a greater degree of order and of decency in public affairs than that which he shows in his own private concerns, which ought indeed to be the constant gauge of his capacity. If he is too fond of the gaming-table, of the wine-glass, and of frivolous amusements, he is not to be entrusted with the discharge of high diplomatic duty, for he will be so unreliable that at moments when he seeks the satisfaction of his ill-regulated desires he will be prepared to sell the highest secrets of his master.

The Cool Head. A man who is naturally violent and easily carried away is ill fitted for the conduct of negotiations ; it is almost impossible for him to be master of him-

34

self at those critical moments and unforeseen occasions when the command of one's temper is of importance, especially at the acute moments of diplomatic controversy when a choleric word may poison the minds of those with whom negotiations are in progress. It is also difficult for any man who is easily irritated to remain master of his own secret ; for, when his anger is aroused, he will allow words to escape him from which an adroit hearer will easily divine the essence of his thought, and thus lead to the ruin of his plans.

Before his elevation to the cardinalate, Cardinal Mazarin was sent on an important mission to the Duke of Feria, Governor of Milan. He was charged to discover the true feelings of the Duke on a certain matter, and he had the cunning to inflame the Duke's anger and thus to discover what he would never have known if the Duke himself had maintained a wise hold over his feelings. The Cardinal indeed had made himself absolute master of all the outward effects which passion usually produces, so much so that neither in his speech nor by the least change in his countenance could one discover his real thought; and this quality which he possessed in so high a degree contributed largely to make him one of the greatest negotiators of his time.

A man who is master of himself and always acts with *sang-froid* has a great advantage over him who *Spanish and Italian Characters.*

is of a lively and easily inflamed nature. One may say indeed that they do not fight with equal arms ; for in order to succeed in this kind of work, one must rather listen than speak ; and the phlegmatic temper, self-restraint, a faultless discretion and a patience which no trial can break down—these are the servants of success. Indeed the last of these qualities, namely patience, is one of the advantages which the Spanish nation has over our own ; for we are naturally lively, and have hardly embarked on one affair before we desire the end in order to embark on another, thus betraying a restlessness which continually seeks new aims. Whereas it has been remarked that a Spanish diplomatist never acts with haste, that he never thinks of bringing a negotiation to an end simply from *ennui*, but to finish it with advantage and to profit from all the favourable conjunctures which present themselves, amongst which our impatience is his advantage. Italy has also produced a large number of excellent negotiators who have contributed much to the high prestige and temporal power of the Court of Rome, even to the point at which we now see it. And we ourselves have the same superiority in the art of negotiation over other northern nations which the Spaniards and Italians have over us, from which it might appear that the degree of intelligence varies in Europe with the degree of warmth of its different climates. Now from all this it follows that a man who by nature is strange, inconstant, and ruled by his own humours and passions, should not enter the profession of diplomacy, but should go to the wars. For as war destroys a great number of those who engage in it, she is not so delicate in the choice of her subjects; she resembles those good stomachs which can digest and assimilate with equal ease every kind of nourishment that is given them—not indeed that a man must not have high and excellent qualities before he can become a good general, but because there are so many degrees of capacity in the army that he who has not sufficient intelligence to arrive at the highest remains half-way and may become a good subaltern or other officer whose service is useful in his own sphere. But it is not the same with a negotiator—if he is not adapted to his function he will often ruin everything that is put under his charge and stain the good name of his master with irreparable prejudice.

Not only must the negotiator be free from way- *Adaptability.* ward humours and fantasies, but he must know how to suffer fools gladly, how to accommodate himself to the changing humours of others. He must indeed be like Proteus of the fable, always ready to take a different figure and posture according to occasion and need. Let him be gay and agreeable with young princes still in the full enjoyment of daily pleasures ; let him be sage and full of counsel with those of more serious years, and in everything let all his attention and care, all his zeal and even his enjoyments and diversions, tend to the one sole aim, which is to bring to success the great business in his charge. Thus it will not always be enough that he should execute the exact letter of his instruction ; his zeal and intelligence should combine how he may profit from all favoured conjunctures that present themselves, and even should be able to create such favourable moments by which the advantage of his prince may be served. There are even pressing and important occasions where he is compelled to make a decision on the spot, to undertake certain *démarches* without waiting for the orders of his master which could not arrive in time. But then he must have sufficient penetration to foresee all the results of his own action, and it were well also if he had acquired beforehand that degree of confidence from his own prince which is commonly founded on a proved capacity of good services. He may thus assure himself in moments of sudden decision that he retains the confidence of his prince and that his past success will plead in favour of his present actions. In the absence of such conditions he would be a bold negotiator indeed who entered into engagements

38

in his master's name without express order on his master's part. But on a pressing occasion he can hold such a thing as eventually to be concluded with advantage to his prince, or at least he may be able to prevent the matter in question from turning to his disadvantage until he shall have received orders from him.

It is well that with all these qualities a negotiator, *Wealth, Birth* and especially one who bears the title of ambas- *and Breeding.* sador, should be rich in order to be able to maintain the necessary expenses of his office ; but a wise prince will not fall into the fault common to many princes, namely that of regarding wealth as the first and most necessary quality in an ambassador. Indeed he will serve his own interests much better by choosing an able negotiator of mediocre fortune than one endowed with all the wealth of the Indies but possessing a small intelligence, for it is obvious that the rich man may not know the true use of riches, whereas the able man will assuredly know how to employ his own ability. And the prince should further remember that it is within his power to equip the able man with all the necessary means, but that it is not in his power to endow with intelligence one who does not possess it.

It is also desirable that an ambassador should be a man of birth and breeding, especially if he is employed in any of the principal courts of Europe,

39

and it is by no means a negligible factor that he should have a noble presence and a handsome face, which undoubtedly are among the means which easily please mankind. An evil-looking person, as General Philopoemen said, will receive many in-sults and suffer much trouble, like the man who was made to hew wood and draw water because he looked like a slave. There are of course missions sent on special occasions where nothing is needed but a great name and the prestige of high birth—as, for instance, in the ceremonial occasions of a mar-riage, or baptism, or the offer of good wishes on the accession of a sovereign to the throne; but when the negotiation concerns important affairs it must be entrusted to a man, not to a gaudy image, unless indeed the image be a puppet in the hands of some crafty colleague who, while possessing the whole secret of negotiation and keeping in his hands all the threads of its designs, leaves the actual public appearance to the ignorant but high-born gentleman whose sole trouble is to maintain a fine table and a magnificent equipage.

The Knowledge Necessary to a Negotiator.

A man born to diplomacy and feeling himself called to the practice of negotiation must commence his studies by a careful examination of the position of various European states, of the principal interests which govern their action, which divide them from one another, of the diverse forms of government

40

which prevail in different parts, and of the character of those princes, soldiers, and ministers who stand in positions of authority. In order to master the detail of such knowledge he must have an understanding of the material power, the revenues, and the whole dominion of each prince or each republic. He must understand the limits of territorial sovereignty ; he must inform himself of the manner in which the government was originally established ; of the claims which each sovereign makes upon parts which he does not possess ; for these ambitions are the very material of negotiation on those occasions when a favourable turn of events prompts the ambitious sovereign to hope that a long-cherished desire may be realised ; and, finally, the negotiator must be able to make a clear distinction between the rights and claims which are founded on treaty obligation and those which rest upon pure force alone. For his own instruction he must read with the most attentive care all public treaties, both general and particular, which have been made between the princes and states of Europe and in our time ; he should consider the treaties concluded between France and the House of Austria as those which offer the principal form and model for the conduct of all the public affairs of Christendom on account of the network of liaisons with other sovereigns which surrounds these two great Powers. And since their disputes took their origin in the relations and treaties existing between the King Louis xi. and Charles, the last Duke of Burgundy, from whom the House of Austria descends, it is vital that the negotiator of our time should be well acquainted with all the treaties made at that period and since ; but especially all those which have been concluded between the principal Powers of Europe beginning with the Treaty of Westphalia right up to the present time.

Europe is his Province. Let him also study with understanding and open eye the modern history of Europe. Let him read the memoirs of great men, the instructions and despatches of all our ablest negotiators, both those which are printed in public books and those which are stored in manuscripts in our Office of Public Records, for these documents treat of great affairs, and the reading of them will convey not only facts which are important for the making of history, but also a sense of the true atmosphere of negotiation, and will thus help to form the mind of him who reads them and give him some clue to guide him in similar occasions on his own career. One of the most profitable readings that I know for this purpose is the despatch of Cardinal d'Ossat, of whose letters I make bold to say, for a man entering upon negotiation, what Horace said to the poets of his time regarding the works of Homer : That he should have them in his hands night and day if he desires perfection in his own art. In a simple and modest manner the despatches of this Cardinal reveal the force and the address which were his great merit, and which, in spite of the antiquity of his style, still give keen pleasure to those who have a taste for good diplomatic writing. One may see thus how by his ability alone, without the assistance of noble birth, title, or other character than that of agent of his queen, Louise de Vaudemont, widow of King Henry III., he was able gradually to conduct the high enterprise of reconciling King Henry the Great with the Holy See after the most famous ambassadors of the time had failed in it ; with what dexterity he escaped all the pitfalls laid for him by the Roman Court, and all the traps which the House of Austria, then at the height of its power, devised for his undoing. The reader will marvel, as he turns each page, how nothing escaped his penetrating eye. He will find even the least movements of Pope Clement VIII. and his nephew the Cardinal recorded with care. He will see how Monseigneur d'Ossat profited by everything, how he is firm as a rock when necessity demands, supple as a willow at another moment, and how he possessed the supreme art of making every man offer him as a gift that which it was his chief design to secure.

Then again in the collection of manuscript despatches regarding the negotiations of Münster, as well as in the memoirs of Cardinal Mazarin, we may read the instructions to the French plenipotentiary, which are indeed masterpieces of their kind, for in them the Cardinal examines the interests of each European Power. He suggests overtures and expedients for adjusting their differences with a capacity and a clearness of view which is altogether surprising, and that in a language which was not his own. His despatches on the Peace of the Pyrenees, by means of which he conveyed to the King the results of his conferences with Don Louis Dharo, Prime Minister of Spain, have also a beauty of their own. We recognise in them also the superiority of his genius and the easy ascendancy which he had gained over the spirit of the Spanish minister with whom he was dealing. There are also other manuscript despatches which deserve recognition. They are to be found in great numbers in the Royal Library and in other collections of books, as, for instance, those of De Noailles, Bishop of Acs, and of Montluc, Bishop of Valence, in which one may also read the authentic account of two noble and able men. We have, too, the letters of President Jeannin, a man of great common sense and solid judgment, who contributed largely to the consolidation of the young Republic of the

NEGOTIATING WITH PRINCES

United Provinces by the twelve years' truce which he prepared, and by the wise counsels which he gave touching all matters of government in that Republic. The reading of such letters as his is well designed to form the judgment of him who will consent to read with intelligent care.

In order to understand the principal interest of European princes, the negotiator must add to the knowledge which we have just been describing *Dynastic Liaisons.* that of dynastic genealogies, so that he may know all the connections and alliances, by marriage and otherwise, between different princes, for these liaisons are often found to be the principal causes of conflict and even of war. He must also know the laws and established customs of the different countries, especially in all matters relating to the succession to the throne and the prevailing habits of the court. The study of the form of government existing in each country is very necessary to the diplomatist, and he should not wait until his arrival in a foreign country to study these questions ; he should prepare himself beforehand, for, unless he is equipped with a certain measure of this knowledge, he will be like a man at sea without a compass. Our own negotiators, who have never travelled before taking up some foreign post and who therefore know nothing of these questions, are usually so saturated in our own national customs and habits as to think that those of all other nations must resemble them; the truth being that the authority which one king has within his kingdom in no way resembles that of the neighbouring monarch, although the superficial likeness between royalty in every country is obvious to every eye.

England and Poland. There are, for instance, countries where it is not enough to be in agreement with the prince and his ministers, because there are other parties who share the national sovereignty with him and who have the power to resist his decisions or to make him change them. Of this state of affairs we have an excellent example in England, where the authority of Parliament frequently obliges the King to make peace or war against his own wish; or again in Poland, where the general Diets have an even more extended power, in which one single vote in the Diet may bring to nought the all but unanimous resolution of the assembly itself, and thus not only defeat the deliberations of that assembly but bring to nought the policy of the King and of the Senate. Therefore the good negotiator in such a country will know where to find the balance of domestic power in order to profit by it when occasion offers.

Besides the general public interests of the state there are private and personal interests and ruling passions in princes and in their ministers or favourites, which often play a determining part in

46

the direction of public policy. It is therefore necessary for the negotiator to inform himself of the nature of these private interests and passions influencing the spirits of those with whom he has to negotiate, in order that he may guide his action by this knowledge either in flattering their passions, which is the easiest way, or by somehow finding means to deflect such personages from their original intentions and engagements and cause them to adopt a new line of policy. Such an enterprise carried to success would indeed be a masterpiece of negotiation.

That great man, the Duc de Rohan, tells us in *Testimony of the Duc de Rohan.* the treatise which he wrote upon the interests of European sovereigns, that the sovereigns rule the people and that interest rules the sovereign ; but we may add that the passions of princes and of their ministers often overrule their interests. We have seen many cases in which monarchs have entered engagements most prejudicial to themselves and their state under the influence of passion. There need be no surprise on this account, for the nations themselves are not free from this error, and are prepared to ruin themselves in order to satisfy hatred, vengeance, and jealousy, the satisfaction of which is often antagonistic to their veritable interests. Without recourse to ancient history it would be easy to prove by modern examples

47

that men do not act upon firm and stable maxims of conduct ; that as a rule they are governed by passion and temperament more than by reason. The bearing of this knowledge upon diplomacy is that since the passion and caprice of men in authority so largely influence the destiny of their subjects, it is the duty of the able negotiator to inform himself as accurately as possible regarding the inclination, state of mind, and the plans of men in authority in order that this information may be placed at the service of his master's interests. And we may be sure that a negotiator who has not laboured to acquire a fund of this general and particular information will reason falsely regarding events, affairs of state, and men, and is liable to make false estimates and give dangerous advice to the prince who employs him. Such knowledge is not to be found in books alone ; it is more easily to be gathered by personal communication with those engaged in public service and by foreign travel, for, however profoundly one may have studied the customs, the policy, or the passions of those who govern in foreign states, everything will appear differently when examined close at hand, and it is impossible to form a just notion of the true character of things except by first-hand acquaintance.

Importance of Foreign Travel. It is therefore desirable that before entering the profession of diplomacy the young man should have travelled to the principal courts of Europe, not merely like those young persons who on leaving the academy or college go to Rome to see the beautiful palaces and the ancient ruins, or to Venice to enjoy the opera and the courtesans; he should indeed embark on his travels at a somewhat riper age when he is more capable of reflection and of appreciating the form and spirit of government in each country, and of studying the merits and faults of princes and ministers—doing all this with the deliberate design of returning to these countries at a future day with profit to himself and his master. Travel conducted on these lines obliges the traveller to keep a vigilant eye upon everything that comes under his notice. It would be well that in certain cases they should accompany the King's ambassadors or envoys as travelling companions after the manner of the Spaniards and the Italians, who regard it as an honour to accompany the ministers of the Crown on their diplomatic journeys. There is nothing better calculated for instruction upon the manner of events in foreign countries or for the training of a young man to represent his own country abroad.

It is highly desirable that such novices in diplo- *Foreign* macy should learn foreign languages, for thus they *Languages Indispensable.* will be protected from the bad faith or the ignorance of interpreters, and from the grave embarrass-

49

ment of having to use them for the purpose of
audiences with the sovereign. It is obvious, too,
that an interpreter may be a betrayer of secrets.
Every one who enters the profession of diplomacy
should know the German, Italian, and Spanish
languages as well as the Latin, ignorance of which
would be a disgrace and a shame to any public man,
for it is the common language of all Christian nations.
It is also very useful and fitting for the diplomat,
on whom grave national responsibility rests, to have
such a general knowledge of science as may tend
to the development of his understanding, but he
must be master of his scientific knowledge and
must not be consumed by it. He must give
science the place which it deserves, and must not
merely consider it as a reason for pride or for contempt of those who do not possess it. While devot-
ing himself to this study with care and attention he
must not become engrossed in it, for he who enters
the public service of his King must consider that
he is destined for action and not for academic study
in his closet; and his principal care must be to
instruct himself regarding all that may affect the
lives of living men rather than the study of the dead.
His professional aim is to penetrate the secrets and
hearts of men; to learn the art of handling them
in such a manner as to make them serve the great
ends of his royal master.

NEGOTIATING WITH PRINCES

If one could establish a rule in France that no *A Rule for the* one should be employed in negotiation until he *Diplomatic Service.* had passed some such apprenticeship as this, and had shown his capacity to profit by study and travel in rendering a good account of the countries which he had seen ; and, further, if one could also establish the rule in the same manner that no high command in the army can be entrusted to an officer who has not made many campaigns, we should be more confident that the King would be well served in his negotiations, and that by these means he would be able to raise up around him a large number of reliable negotiators. This is a most desirable end, for as we have seen there are many actions in which the perfect practice of the art of negotiation is not less useful than that of war, and that in France at the present time the art of war stands far above that of diplomacy in public esteem.

But as men are not yet perfect enough to serve *Rewards for* without hope of reward, it is desirable that there *Service.* should be in France a higher degree of honour and fortune for those who have deserved well of their country in diplomacy, as indeed there are in many other courts in Europe where the King's subjects have gained high distinction in that branch of the public service. There are indeed countries in which the distinguished diplomatist may hope to reach the highest place and most exalted dignities in the realm, by which means we in France may learn to raise the profession of diplomacy to that degree of public recognition which it deserves, and from which the service of the King and the greatness of the kingdom must certainly profit.

On the Choice of Diplomatists. The right choice of negotiators depends upon their personal quality, their training, and to some extent their fortune, and as the endowments of mankind vary in a wide degree, so it is found that one kind will fit better into the office of diplomacy than another. At the same time there are men of such wide capacity that they can be safely employed in very different enterprises, and even in very different countries. Such men by their adaptability, by the receptiveness of their nature, and the pliancy of their character are well fitted for the province of diplomacy, and quickly accommodate themselves to new surroundings. It should be the aim of all governments to develop a whole race of such men from whose ranks they may draw their diplomatic agents. It is true that in any one generation there will only be a few geniuses of the first order, and that the rank and file of the diplomatic service will be composed of persons of a more limited type, in which case it is all the more incumbent upon the Minister for Foreign Affairs to exercise the greatest care in assigning ambassadors to foreign posts. He must therefore be well acquainted with the whole service in order to know where to lay his hand upon the appropriate person for any given enterprise.

There are, broadly speaking, three principal human professions. The first is the Ecclesiastical; the second is that of the Gentlemen of the Sword, which besides those actually serving in the army includes courtiers and squires and other ranks of gentlemen in his Majesty's service; and the third is the profession of the Law, whose devotees in France are called ' Gentlemen of the Cloth.' There are not many countries where ecclesiastics can be employed in diplomacy, for one cannot properly send them to heretical or infidel countries. At Rome, which appears to be their home, their attachment to the Pope, and their desire to receive honours from him as well as other benefits which depend upon service at his Court, undoubtedly places them under the suspicion of following too closely the Jesuitical maxims which rule papal policy, and often operate to the prejudice of the temporal power of other kings. *The Three Professions.*

The Republic of Venice has shown much wisdom in this matter, for she is so convinced of the partiality of Venetian prelates towards the Holy See that not only does she exclude them from all diplomatic offices in connection with the Court of Rome, but she actually excludes them from all *The Example of Venice.*

53

discussion of the political relation between Venice
and Rome. It is obvious indeed to all that a digni-
tary of the Church owes a divided allegiance, and
it seems probable that where his loyalty to the
Church conflicts with his loyalty to his sovereign,
the former is likely to prevail. Indeed, the more
closely one examines the proper duties of a bishop,
for instance, the more firmly convinced does one
become that these duties are not compatible with
those of an ambassador ; for on the one hand it is
not fitting that a minister of religion should run
about the world and thus neglect those duties
which should have first claim upon him, and on the
other, as we have seen, political and ecclesiastical
allegiance may come into collision with disastrous
results. And surely a state must be poorly endowed with men if it can find nowhere but in the
Church a sufficiency of adept diplomatists. I am
the last to dispute the great services which certain
prelates have rendered to the French state in the
past, but I consider it useful to be guided as a
general rule by the foregoing considerations.

*The Ambas-
sador a Man
of Peace.*
The best diplomatist will usually be found to be
a man of good birth, sometimes a knight trained
to the profession of arms, and it has occasionally
been found that a good general officer has served
with success as an ambassador, especially at a time
when the military affairs of either state were pro-

minent subjects of negotiation. But diplomacy is not to be regarded as linked with war, for, although war arises out of policy, it is to be regarded as nothing more than a means to an end in itself. Therefore the ambassador should be a man of peace ; for in most cases, and certainly wherever the foreign court is inclined towards peace, it is best to send a diplomatist who works by persuasion and is an adept in winning the good graces of those around him. In either case it will be observed that the public interests will be best served by appointing a professional diplomatist who by long experience has acquired a high aptitude for the peculiar office of diplomacy. Neither the soldier nor the courtier can hope to discharge the duties of diplomacy with success unless they have taken pains to instruct themselves in public policy, and in all that region of knowledge which I have already described as necessary for the negotiator.

It is true that sometimes a lawyer diplomat has *Lawyer* made a great success of negotiation, especially in *Diplomats.* countries where the final responsibility for public policy lay with public assemblies which could be moved by adroit speech, but in general the training of a lawyer breeds habits and dispositions of mind which are not favourable to the practice of diplomacy. And though it be true that success in the law-courts depends largely upon a knowledge of human nature and an ability to exploit it—both of which are factors in diplomacy—it is none the less true that the occupation of the lawyer, which is to split hairs about nothing, is not a good preparation for the treatment of grave public affairs in the region of diplomacy. If this be true of the advocate or barrister, it is still more true of the magistrate and judge. The habit of mind engendered by presiding over a court of law, in which the judge himself is supreme, tends to exclude those faculties of suppleness and adaptability which are necessary in diplomacy, and the almost ludicrous assumption of dignity by a judge would certainly appear as arrogance in diplomatic circles. I do not say that there have not been great lawyers and great judges who were endowed with high diplomatic qualities, but again I place these considerations before my readers in the belief that the more closely they are observed the more surely will they lead to efficiency in the diplomatic profession.

Diplomacy demands Professional Training.

Let me further emphasise my conviction, which, alas, is not yet shared even by ministers of state in France, that diplomacy is a profession by itself which deserves the same preparation and assiduity of attention that men give to other recognised professions. The qualities of a diplomatist and the knowledge necessary to him cannot, indeed, all be

56

acquired. The diplomatic genius is born, not made. But there are many qualities which may be developed with practice, and the greater part of the necessary knowledge can only be acquired by constant application to the subject. In this sense diplomacy is certainly a profession itself capable of occupying a man's whole career, and those who think to embark upon a diplomatic mission as a pleasant diversion from their common task only prepare disappointment for themselves and disaster for the cause which they serve. The veriest fool would not entrust the command of an army to a man whose sole badge of merit was his successful eloquence in a court of law or his adroit practice of the courtier's art in the palace. All are agreed that military command must be earned by long service in the army. In the same manner it should be regarded as folly to entrust the conduct of negotiations to an untrained amateur unless he has conspicuously shown in some other walk of life the qualities and knowledge necessary for the practice of diplomacy.

It often happens that there are men in public life *Fatality of* who have won a reputation for themselves without *Bad Appointments.* earning it. That is possible in the political world, which has many camp followers and hangers-on of all kinds, and there is always a risk that a minister in search of an ambassador for a foreign post will use the occasion to pay an old debt to some powerful patrician family or to some blackmailer behind the scenes. Those who take the responsibility of appointing to high diplomatic offices persons of this character are responsible before God and man for all the injuries which may thereby accrue to the public interest. It cannot be too plainly stated that, while in many cases where trouble has arisen the negotiator himself is to blame, the true responsibility must rest with the minister at home, who not only devises the policy itself but chooses the instruments of it. It is therefore one of the highest maxims of good government that the public interest must be supreme, and that therefore both the prince himself and his ministers must steel themselves to resist the pressure of friends and relations who seek employment for unworthy persons. In diplomacy, above all things, since peace and war and the welfare of nations depend upon it, the best minds, the most sagacious and instructed of public servants should be appointed to the principal foreign posts regardless of the personal affairs of the prince himself or the party attachments of the chosen ambassadors.

'We have fools in Florence, but we do not export them.'

Nothing should stand in the way of the creation of a vigilant, sagacious, and high-minded diplomatic service. Men of small minds should content themselves with employment at home, where their errors may easily be repaired, for errors committed abroad are too often irreparable. The late Duke of Tuscany, who was a remarkably wise and enlightened prince, once complained to the Venetian ambassador, who stayed over-night with him on his journey to Rome, that the Republic of Venice had sent as resident at his court a person of no value, possessing neither judgment nor knowledge, nor even any attractive personal quality. ' I am not surprised,' said the ambassador in reply ; ' we have many fools in Venice.' Whereupon the Grand Duke retorted : 'We also have fools in Florence, but we take care not to export them.'

The Duke's remarks show how important it is in every respect to choose the right man for the diplomatic service, and, in order to give the Foreign Minister an adequate freedom of choice, his diplomatic service should contain men of different characters and a wide variety of accomplishments. Thus he will not be compelled to send an unsuitable man merely because he was the only one available. He should have most careful regard in this choice to the type of government and the religion which prevails in the foreign country in question. There used to be a jest current in Paris on this very subject. The French King had sent a bishop to Constantinople and an heretic to Rome, and it was said that the one had gone to convert the

Grand Turk and the other to be converted by the Pope!

Apart from any higher consideration, it is a mere measure of prudence to avoid sending an envoy who may be presumed to be a *persona ingrata* at the foreign court, for he will certainly, whether he will or not, create a prejudice against his own country and will be quite unable to meet his competitors in diplomacy on equal terms, for he will start with the handicap of unpopularity. The Foreign Minister, therefore, should not wait until matters go wrong at a foreign capital, but should be in a position, when each appointment is made, to know the character of the new ambassador, and thus to veto a bad appointment. This, alas, is not by any means always the case. I do not need to enter upon a minute examination of the faults to avoid and the virtues to encourage in the complete diplomat. I have already said enough to show where my opinion lies in a general way. I will only add one or two further considerations. I said a few moments ago that loose living is a great handicap in diplomacy ; but, since there is no rule which has not some exception, let me point out that a too abstemious negotiator will miss many opportunities of finding out what is going on. Especially in the northern countries the diplomat who loves a glass will quickly make friends among ministers, though, to be sure, he should drink in such a manner as not to lose control of his own faculties while endeavouring to loosen the self-control of others.

In diplomacy a nation is judged by its ministers, *The Nation* and its whole reputation may rest upon the popu-*judged by its Servants.* larity or unpopularity of an ambassador. In this respect the personal conduct of the ambassador and his staff is almost as important as the policy with which he is charged, for the success of the policy will depend largely upon the actual relations which exist between the two nations. The ambassador is, as it were, the very embodiment of these relations, and if a proper adept in his profession will know how to turn every occasion to advantage. I need not repeat my tale of the qualities and practices by which such advantage may be drawn from the current of events, but I may perhaps point out that obviously men of birth and breeding are better able to discharge the kind of function which I have described. Their rank will command a certain respect, and the qualities usually inherited by those of good birth should stand them in good stead at a foreign court. At the same time such qualities must not be regarded as more than a foundation. They cannot in themselves equip a diplomatist for his office. He must by assiduous application acquire the other necessary qualities, for there is no man more liable to suspicion than he who plumes himself on an experience which he does not possess. Further, it is usually unwise to entrust important negotiations to young men, who are commonly presumptuous and vain as well as indiscreet. Old age is equally inappropriate. The best time of life is its prime, in which you find experience, discretion, and moderation, combined with vigour.

Men of Letters. Other things being equal, I prefer a man of letters before one who has not made a habit of study, for his reading will give him a certain equipment which he might otherwise lack. It will adorn his conversation and supply him with the necessary historic setting in which to place his own negotiations; whereas an ignorant man will be able to quote nothing but the will of his master, and will thus present his argument in a naked and unattractive form. It must be obvious that the knowledge gained in a lifetime of reading is an important adjunct in diplomacy, and above all, the reading of history is to be preferred, for without it the negotiator will be unable to understand the meaning of historical allusions made by other diplomatists, and may thus miss the whole point at some important turn in negotiations. And since it is not enough to think aright, the diplomatist must be able to translate his thoughts into the right language, and conversely he must be able to pierce behind the language of others to their true thoughts. It may often happen that an historical allusion will reveal the purpose of a minister's mind far better than any direct argument. Herein lies the importance of culture in diplomacy. The name of orator has sometimes been given to ambassadors because in certain past times they have been in the habit of delivering their instructions in the form of an eloquent address ; but diplomatic eloquence is a very different thing from that of Parliament or the Bar. An ambassador's speeches should contain more sense than words, and he should studiously avoid every affectation. His aim should be to arouse the minds of his hearers by a sympathetic touch, after which it will be easy to deliver his message in an appropriate way. He should therefore at the outset think rather of what is in their minds than of immediately expressing what is in his own. It is in this that true eloquence consists, and indeed the words I have just used are the beginning and end of all diplomacy.

In general his mode of address, whether he speak *The Fitting* to the sovereign or to his ministers, should be *Mode of Address.* moderate and reserved. He should not raise his voice but should maintain the ordinary conversational tone, at once simple and dignified, revealing an innate respect both for his own high office and for the person whom he is addressing. He should, above all things, avoid the prolix, pompous approach which is natural to princes who attach more importance to ceremonial than to the essence of any matter. But if the ambassador be called upon to deliver his message to a Senate or a Parliament, he will bear in mind that the means for gaining the good graces of an individual and of an assembly are by no means the same. In such public speech he may permit himself a certain freedom of rhetoric, but even here he must beware of prolonging his speech beyond a tolerable limit. The reply of the Spartans to ambassadors from the Isle of Samos stands as a warning for all times against prolixity : ' We have forgotten the beginning of your harangue ; we paid no heed to the middle of it, and nothing has given us pleasure in it except the end.' God forbid that any French negotiator should receive so damning a rebuff !

The Well-Stored Mind. Even at the best of times a man of good sense will not rely entirely on his native wit. He will find that knowledge of historical precedents will often act as a lever with which to remove obstacles from his path. Such knowledge of history, and particularly the true aptitude in applying it to current events, cannot be learned except by long experience. Even in those cases where success has attended the efforts of an amateur diplomatist, the example must be regarded as an exception, for it is a commonplace of human experience that skilled work requires a skilled workman. The more important the business on hand, the more vital it is that ministers of state should ensure for themselves the services of trained men. I am well aware that even the greatest courts sometimes neglect this vital precaution, and fill their embassies with improper persons, mainly because the minister or the prince had not sufficient strength of mind to resist appeals made on illegitimate grounds such as that of family influence. It will usually be found that the real expert does not push himself or his claims, and that the superior minds in diplomacy, as in other walks of life, are not found crying their wares at every street corner, but must be sought out with care in their own closets. It is also to be observed that in previous times the profession of diplomacy stood too low in public esteem to attract the services of first-class men—partly because higher emoluments were to be earned elsewhere, and partly on account of the prolonged absence from home which diplomatic service entails.

If diplomacy be a labour in exile, the state should see to it that it is at least an honourable exile. To counteract this drawback, the home government should so reform the system of diplomacy that it may offer attractions to the most ambitious as well as to the most refined spirits. There is no reason *Diplomacy an Honourable Exile.*

why not merely honour but adequate daily recompense for his services should not be offered to the diplomatists from the very beginning of their career. Having regard to the expenses which fall upon the diplomatists of all ranks in their service abroad, and in maintaining the honour of their own profession and their country, the prince will be well advised to pay good salaries and in other ways to mark his esteem of the diplomatic profession. Thus and thus alone can a prince gather round him a diplomatic bodyguard worthy of the name. If he follows this advice, his diplomatic service will quickly outstrip all others and a deeper mutual confidence will arise between himself and his diplomatic agents upon which the success of all his negotiations will rest secure. No diplomatist is less to be envied than he who finds himself at a foreign court bereft of the confidence of his own.

Value of a Well-Equipped Service. Now the equipment of the state in diplomacy will be incomplete unless the diplomatic service contains within its ranks so large a number of practised and seasoned diplomatists that the King may be able to retain several of them at his side as special advisers in foreign affairs. In every campaign the true commander will take as much trouble for his reserves as for his first line of attack, and similarly the position of reserves in diplomacy has a great importance, for it means not only that the Minister

NEGOTIATING WITH PRINCES

for Foreign Affairs will have at his elbow a number of skilled diplomatists to assist him in a moment of crisis, but also that when one of the embassies abroad suddenly falls vacant his choice of a successor will not be too narrowly restricted. He thus will be able to avoid the fatal practice, which has prevailed too often in recent French history, of having to choose an ambassador haphazard at the last moment from among the courtiers and hangers-on at the palace.

The nature of the business on hand must largely govern the choice of the ambassador who is appointed to carry it out, and if the diplomatic service be large enough and varied enough it will certainly contain within its ranks many different characters showing a wide variety of aptitude. Thus in all those secret negotiations which are so necessary in order to prepare the ground for treaties it is often found that the ambassador himself is not the best person to employ. It may be highly embarrassing for him to attempt to combine such secret negotiations with the ordinary duties of his office, and therefore a clever man who is not yet clothed with the prestige of high office is a more proper agent for this kind of secret traffic. The very fact that the high public position of an ambassador is apt to make the court and the general public familiar with his person and his face is certainly a draw-

The Right Man in the Right Place.

67

back to his employment on more secret affairs, and
though it is true, as we have said, that part of the
business of an ambassador is that of an honourable
spy, he should beware of doing any of the spying
himself. Most of the great events in recent diplomatic history have been prepared by ministers sent
in secret. The Peace of Münster, one of the most
intricate negotiations I have ever known, was not
really the work of that vast concourse of ambassadors
and envoys which met there and appended their
signatures to the document. The essential clauses
of that treaty were discussed and drawn up by a
secret agent of Duke Maximilian of Bavaria sitting
at a table in Paris with Cardinal Mazarin. In a
similar fashion the Peace of the Pyrenees was concluded as the result of secret negotiations at Lyons
between Cardinal Mazarin and Pimentel, the
secret envoy of the Spanish King ; and finally, the
Peace of Ryswick, to which I was a party throughout the negotiation, was devised by the same secret
diplomacy before its public ratification in Holland
in the year 1697.

Each Embassy
a Miniature
of the Whole
Service.

Now the bearing of these considerations upon
the organisation of diplomacy is fairly clear. If it is
only a question of maintaining good relations
between one state and another and of rendering a
more or less correct account of all that happens at
a foreign court, a diplomatist with a couple of secre-

taries will suffice, and indeed in ordinary times it is undoubtedly better not to have more than one diplomatist of the same rank at any foreign court. But it is equally obvious that there are occasions when it is of the highest advantage to maintain a more elaborately equipped mission at a foreign court, and even to send two or three diplomatists of higher rank to assist in the conduct of negotiations and in the other activities of diplomacy. This is of course true whenever a peace conference is about to meet, for negotiations of that character require great preparation beforehand, and it would be impossible for a single diplomatist to overtake all the work which is necessary in such circumstances together with the manifold duties of his own office. In a certain sense the embassy itself should be a reproduction in miniature of the whole diplomatic service.

There is undoubtedly room in all the larger em- *Variety of* bassies for a great variety of talent, which will find *Talent.* an appropriate field of action if the head of the mission is wise enough to give the younger men their chance. For instance, it sometimes happens that an embassy will find it is in a country distracted by civil war, and then the best practice of the ambassador will be severely tested. If he has encouraged his juniors to form relationships of various kinds with different parties in the country for the purpose of acquiring information, he will find that on the outbreak even of so distracting a commotion as civil war he has the means within his own embassy of keeping touch with both sides in the dispute. Naturally he will find it a difficult and delicate task not to be embroiled with either side ; but he will certainly find all his previous trouble amply repaid by the fulness of the information which he receives from both sides. On no account should he allow prejudice regarding social rank or political opinion to stand in the way of the formation of useful relations between members of his staff and different parties in the country. He himself is debarred from such action, and indeed if he were alone with nothing but one or two secretaries to assist him, it would be quite impossible for him to know what was passing in either camp, and he would have to rely on second-hand information which he was not in a position to test. Still worse would be his case if, having become the personal friend of the chief of one of the parties, he should find the other party coming into power, and thereafter treating him as an enemy.

Merit the only Standard. Such considerations must ever be borne in mind by the Minister for Foreign Affairs. But least of all men should he be influenced by regard for rank, social station, or political opinion in his choice of attachés and other persons in any rank in diplo-

macy. Especially where he is about to despatch
an embassy to a state under popular government,
he will remember that the ambassador will require
many agents to keep him in touch with all the
different parties. It is therefore to be observed
that those embassies which are sent to popularly
governed states must be chosen with greater care
and equipped with a more varied staff than those
despatched to a foreign court where the government
rests entirely in the hands of the King.

Before discussing in detail the duties of ne- *The Diplo-*
gotiators, I shall describe the different titles which *matic Hier-*
archy:
they receive, and the functions and privileges at- *Ambassadors.*
tached to their office. Negotiators are of two
kinds : of the first and second order. Those of the
first order are Ambassadors Extraordinary and
Ambassadors Ordinary. Those of the second are
Envoys Extraordinary and Residents. Ambassadors extraordinary receive certain honours and
distinctions not accorded to ambassadors ordinary. The ambassadors extraordinary of crowned
heads are lodged and entertained in France for
three days, by order of the King, in residences set
aside for them, while ambassadors ordinary are
not so entertained by the King, though in other
respects they enjoy the same honour and privileges
as the former. These privileges consist in the
enjoyment under international law of immunity

and security, in the right to remain covered before the King in public audiences because they represent their masters, in the privilege of being borne in the King's coach, and of driving their own coaches into the inner court of the Louvre. They have still their own dais in the audience-chamber, while their wives have a seat by the Queen ; and they are permitted to drape the driving seat of their coaches with a special saddle cloth. In France the ambassadors of the Dukes of Savoy enjoyed the same honours as those of the crowned heads of Europe. Abroad the King's ambassadors enjoy different ceremonial rights according to the customs established in different courts. The French ambassador in Rome, for instance, gives his hand to the ambassadors of certain crowned heads and of Venice, but there are certain ambassadors of other sovereigns who do not receive this courtesy, though at other courts it is accorded to them by the French ambassador. The French ambassador takes first rank in all ceremonies in Rome after the ambassador of the Emperor. These two ambassadors receive the same salary, and are treated otherwise on a footing of equality. There are several courts at which the French ambassadors give their hand to certain princes of equality in the country': in Spain, for instance, we find the Grandees ; in London, the Peers of the Realm ;

in Sweden and in Poland the Senators and Grand Officers; but to the negotiators of the rank of envoy this courtesy is not accorded. The King does not send an ambassador to the Electorates of Germany, but conducts his negotiation with them merely by means of envoys.

Envoys extraordinary are public ministers who *Envoys Extraordinary.* do not possess the right of presentation which attaches alone to the title of ambassador, but they enjoy the same security and immunity under the law of nations. They do not make a state entry into a foreign capital in the manner of ambassadors, but are presented in audiences to the King by the diplomatic usher, who fetches them from their private residence in one of the King's coaches; they speak to his Majesty standing and uncovered, the King himself being seated and covered. The Emperor on the other hand receives the envoys of the King standing and covered, and remains in this condition throughout the entire audience, the envoy alone of all those present standing uncovered. . . . The title of plenipotentiary is sometimes given to envoys as well as to ambassadors according to the occasion. For instance, the ministers whom the King maintains at the Diet of Ratisbon receive the title of plenipotentiary although they are not ambassadors. Residents are also public ministers, but this title has been somewhat degraded since the distinction was drawn both at the French Court and at the Court of the Emperor between them and envoys, with the result that nearly all foreign negotiators in France who bore the title of resident have relinquished it by order of their masters, and have assumed that of envoy extraordinary. None the less the title is still found in Rome and in other courts and republics where the residents are treated as envoys.

Secret Envoys. There are certain secret envoys who are only received in private audiences but enjoy the same immunity as public envoys, and from the moment in which they present their credentials are recognised as public ministers. There are also secretaries and agents attached to the court for various forms of public business, but they are not received in audience by the King in France ; they do all their business with the Secretary of State or the Minister for Foreign Affairs, and though themselves not recorded as ministers have also enjoyed the protection and immunity under international law which is accorded to foreign ambassadors. No subject of the King can be received as minister or representative of a foreign prince, nor can they conduct his affairs in France except as agents of the Secretary of State, the only exception being the ambassador from Malta, who is usually a French

Member of the Order, and to whom the King accords the right to remain covered in public audience as representative of the Grand Master of the Order, who himself is recognised as possessing sovereign rights.

Only princes and sovereign states have the right *Agents of* to clothe their messengers with the character of *Small States.* ambassador, envoy, or resident. The agents of small states or of the free states are called deputies ; they are not public ministers, and they are subject to the jurisdiction of the country like any private citizen ; they do not enjoy immunity under the law of nations, though by custom deputies from provinces and from free cities are accorded immunity and security in practice during their deputation as a proof of the good faith of the prince in negotiation. In the same manner private citizens provided with passports may travel free from molestation. There are certain states in Italy which, though neither sovereign Powers nor subject to another sovereign, have yet conserved the right to send deputies with the title of ambassador to the sovereign under whose sway they live. These are the cities of Bologna and Ferrara, which send diplomatic deputations to the Pope in this manner, and the city of Messina, which retained the right of sending ambassadors to the King of Spain before the last rising. There are similarly several Spanish cities which do not now retain this right. These ambassadors of states or subject provinces resemble in some manner those whom the Roman people used to receive from their own free provinces, from the cities and colonies subject to Roman rule, to whom the name of *Legati* was given, a name which still occurs in all Latin diplomatic documents. There are certain free cities, such as Hamburg and Lübeck, which send commissaries to certain princes ; but as a rule they are merely commercial agents engaged upon such matters of business as the purchase and sale of merchandise and the conditions of letters of exchange.

Precedence. Now although the position of an ambassador extraordinary is something more honourable than that of the ambassador ordinary they are practically treated alike if there is an equality between the princes whom they represent. The title of extraordinary gives no other superiority over the ambassador ordinary except in pure matters of precedence. Envoys extraordinary and residents stand in somewhat of the same relation, that is to say, that the resident of a prince of higher rank takes precedence over an envoy extraordinary of a prince of lesser rank. It is not, however, the same between ambassadors and envoys. The envoy of a crowned head must yield the place of honour to the ambassador of a lesser sovereign as in the following example. An envoy of the Emperor at the French Court some years ago took his seat at a public entertainment in the place which was reserved for the ambassador ordinary of the Duke of Savoy, and asserted his right to it on the ground of the difference in rank between their respective masters; but the dispute was decided in favour of the ambassador as holding superior rank without regard to the difference in the rank of their respective princes; and the envoy of the Emperor was obliged to leave the position which he had taken and yield it to the ambassador of Savoy.

The title of excellency has been given to ambassadors extraordinary and ordinary, but it is not accorded to envoys unless they claim it on some other ground, as, for instance, that they are ministers of state or senators, or other high officers at a royal court. This title of excellency is not in common use at the French Court, as it is in Spain, Italy, and Germany, and the kingdoms of the north, and you will only find foreigners in France addressing the King's ministers or other officers of the court with that title. But foreign negotiators of all kinds are addressed by that title as a mark of courtesy to the rank which they hold. *The Title of Excellency.*

The Court of Rome has three different degrees of titles by which to mark the rank of her ministers in foreign courts. The first is that of *Legato a latere,* *Legates, Nuncios, and Internuncios.*

77

the second is that of Ordinary or Extraordinary Nuncio, and the third is the Internuncio. The first of these is always a cardinal, to whom as a rule the Pope gives very wide powers both for the affairs of papal diplomacy and for the administration of dispensations and other privileges of the Holy See. They are received at all Catholic Courts with extraordinary honours : in France at their presentation they are attended by the princes of the blood ; they remain seated and covered in audience with the King, whereas both ambassadors and even papal nuncios speak to him standing. These legates have a further honour accorded neither to nuncios nor ambassadors in France, namely the right to eat at the King's table at the banquet of reception given by his Majesty in their honour. The Cross is carried before them to mark their ecclesiastical jurisdiction, which, however, is strictly limited in France, and is recognised in certain specified cases for the verification of Papal Bulls at the Parliament of Paris, to which they must present them before attempting to put them into force. Nuncios both ordinary and extraordinary are usually prelates of the rank of archbishop or bishop. They are received and presented by a prince of the royal blood at their first and final audiences with the King, no difference being made between the nuncio extraordinary and the nuncio ordinary except that the former takes precedence of the latter if there are two present in the same Chamber. None the less the prelates of the Court of Rome prefer the title of nuncio ordinary at the Courts of France, Spain, and of the Emperor, because it is a shorter and a surer road to the cardinal's hat, which is the goal of their aspirations. As regards their appointment, when the Pope desires to send a nuncio ordinary to the French Court, he presents the French ambassador in Rome with a list of several dignitaries of the Church, from which the King may exclude those who are not agreeable to him. The papal nuncios in France give their hand to the Secretary of State for Foreign Affairs, but not to bishops or archbishops received on ceremonial vists. They have no ecclesiastical jurisdiction in France in the sense in which they possess it in Vienna, in Spain, in Portugal, in Poland, and in many other Catholic states, where they are recognised as valid judges in various cases, and have the power of dispensation in the same way as the archbishops or the diocesan bishop. In France they are only entitled to receive the confession of faith of those whom the King has nominated to bishoprics and to inquire regarding their life and habits.

Ambassadors, envoys, and residents all possess *Diplomatic* the right to exercise freely the religion of their *Privileges.* King, and to admit to such ordinances their own nationals living in the foreign country. In matters of law diplomatists of rank are not subject to the jurisdiction of the judges of that foreign country where they reside, and both they and their household enjoy what is called extra-territoriality, their embassy being regarded as it were the house of the King himself, and as being an asylum for his nationals. But this privilege carries its corresponding duty. No blame can be too severe for those ministers abroad who abuse this right of asylum in sheltering under their roof evilly disposed persons, either those condemned to death for crime, or those who are engaged upon any business which renders them unworthy of the protection of the King. The sagacious diplomat will not compromise the authority of his master for any such odious reason as the attempt to confer immunity upon a criminal. It must suffice for him that his own right of asylum is kept inviolate, and he must never employ it except on extraordinary occasions in his master's service, and never indeed for his own private profit. On the other hand, the King must expressly forbid his judges, bailiffs, or private citizens to violate the law of nations in the person of a foreign envoy, who is always recognised as under the protection of international law. And whereever insult is offered to a foreign envoy, the prince himself must repair it without fail in the same manner in which he would expect return for a like insult to his own minister abroad.

It sometimes occurs that ministers abuse the right *Abuse of* of free passage, which they possess for their own *Immunity.* provisions and the equipment necessary for their establishment, to carry on a clandestine trade from which they draw large profits by lending their name to fraud. This kind of profit is utterly unworthy of the public minister, and makes his name stink in the nostrils of the King to whom he is sent as well as to his own prince. A wise minister may be well content to enjoy the large privileges to which he is entitled in every foreign country without attempting to abuse them for his own private profit, or by countenancing any fraud which is committed under the protection of his name. The Spanish Government was obliged a few years ago severely to regulate these privileges for all foreign envoys residing in Madrid, and the Republic of Genoa found it necessary to adopt the same somewhat humiliating precautions in order to prevent diplomatists from engaging in illicit traffic The privileges conferred by the law of nations upon envoys abroad permit full freedom in their proper duty of labouring to discover all that passes in the council-chamber of his Majesty, and to take steps to form close relations with those best able to supply this information, but they are not to be interpreted as covering any attempt to form a conspiracy against the public peace ; for the same international right which covers the person of a diplomatist must also be held to cover the peace and security of the kingdom to which he is accredited. Therefore the diplomatist will be on his guard against any action which may seem to lend the authority of his name or office to revolutionary plots or to other hostile acts against the peace of the realm. Should he neglect this precaution, he may find himself treated as an enemy.

Henry IV. and the Duke of Savoy.
Charles Emanuel the first Duke of Savoy maintained certain connections in France with some of the principal peers at the Court of Henry IV., and engaged with them in plots and cabals. He attended the French Court under the pretext of paying his respects to the King, but in reality with the intention of spreading his own influence and fortifying his own designs, which were to prevent Henry IV. from forcing him to restore the Marquisate of Saluse which he had usurped. The King discovered the Duke's intrigue, and held a cabinet meeting on the matter. The Council was of opinion that the Duke had come under a false show of friendship in order to disturb the peace of the realm, that the King was therefore fully within his rights in laying hands upon him as upon an enemy, that in consequence of his own acts the

82

Duke could claim no immunity, and that therefore the King would be justified in preventing him from leaving France until he had restored the marquisate in question. But the King did not agree with his ministers, but said : ' The Duke came to visit me on my parole. If he has failed in his duty I do not wish to imitate so evil an example, and I have so fine a precedent in my own house that I am compelled to follow it rather than to follow the Duke.' In this he spoke of Francis I., who in a similar case gave the Emperor Charles v. a free passage through France without insisting that he should relinquish the Duchy of Milan ; and although several of the King's counsellors at that time were of opinion that he should profit by the opportunity to compel the Emperor to restore the duchy, which indeed he had several times promised to do, Francis I. preferred to maintain his own honour above every other interest. Henry IV. acted on the same principle ; he permitted the Duke of Savoy to depart unmolested after heaping honours and entertainments upon him, but the moment the Duke had returned to his own Court the King demanded the restitution of the Marquisate of Saluse according to his promise. The Duke refused, whereupon the King invaded Savoy, occupied the whole duchy, and compelled him to keep his word, not only to the extent of the marquisate but of several other parts which he was compelled to cede to the King by a treaty concluded at Lyons, on the 17th January 1601.

Reparation for Abuse of Immunity. Those who think that one may lay forcible hands upon a sovereign who has broken his word will easily persuade themselves that in a similar case no international law can protect the person of a mere minister ; but those who are really well instructed in the law of nations and in the question of sovereign rights are of opinion that a foreign envoy being subject to the laws of the country where he lives it is not possible to put into motion against him the machinery of domestic justice, that the only redress for wrongs done by him is an appeal to his master, and that if his master refuses reparation the responsibility must lie with him and not on his minister abroad who merely executes his order. This privilege, be it remembered, extends not merely to the ambassadors themselves but often to their servants, as is illustrated in the following example.

The Merargue Conspiracy. King Henry IV., whom one may take as a model for princes, was warned by the Duke de Guise of the Merargue Conspiracy in which a Provencal squire named Merargue had entered into an arrangement with Dom Balthazar de Zuniga, the Spanish ambassador, to hand over the city of Marseilles to the Spaniards at a moment of profound peace.   The

NEGOTIATING WITH PRINCES

King arrested not only Merargue, but also the private secretary to the Spanish ambassador, a man named Bruneau. Both were convicted of conspiracy. Merargue was executed, and the King handed over the private secretary to his own ambassador, saying that he would be glad to see Bruneau sent across the frontier, though he himself reserved the right to demand satisfaction from the Spanish King for Bruneau's misdemeanour.

Now if princes had the right to proceed against *Immunity a* foreign envoys at their courts, the latter would *Function of* never feel themselves secure, because then it would *Sovereignty.* be easy to get rid of any of them on flimsy pretexts, and the precedent once set up in a good case would surely be followed in many cases where nothing but idle suspicion could be brought against the envoy in question. This indeed would be the end of all diplomacy. Of course it is true that a minister who breaks faith cannot expect others to keep faith with him, especially if he is engaged upon conspiracies or any of those practices against the prince and safety of the realm of which I have spoken. But even in such a case the wise prince will not break the law of nations, which should always be respected. He will rather use his good offices at the court whence the erring envoy came in order to have him withdrawn. At the same time it is always permissible to place a watch upon a faithless

85

ambassador, in order to hinder him in practices which would otherwise do harm to the state, and of course on the other part a wise ambassador will certainly avoid falling into such intrigues, for the very protection which he enjoys under the law of nations is a guarantee of his person and of his good behaviour. Benefits under it are reciprocal, and the reciprocal duties which it imposes should be scrupulously observed. If they are not, no law of nations can guarantee an intriguing ambassador for ever against the fury of the populace once they are aroused by suspicion.

Its Abuse undermines True Diplomacy.

On all these grounds the minister is to be pitied who receives commands from his master to form cabals in a foreign state, and he will need all his skill and courage to carry out such commands without being trapped in the process. It has been truly said that there is no service which a prince may not expect from good subjects and faithful ministers, but such obedience cannot be held to cover any action against the laws of God or of justice, which do not countenance for one moment attempts on the life of a prince, or against the security of the state, or any other unfriendly act committed under cover of the protecting title of ambassador. A good ambassador will always discourage plans of this kind, and if his master persists in them he may and should demand his recall, and retire into obscurity, jealously guarding his sovereign's evil secret. In justice to most reigning sovereigns it must be said that few of them engage in designs of this kind. The vast majority of intrigues and cabals are made in their name in foreign states, or are suggested to them by their ministers or by astute diplomatists, who undertake to carry them out, and through them to confer great benefits upon the prince himself. But these diplomatists are often the first to fall into traps set by their own hand, and are then objects of pity to no man. Numerous examples of this kind can be quoted, and I think no one will challenge the truth of my observation when I say that in nine cases out of ten diplomatists who give such advice are actuated more by personal ambition or petty spite than by the true interests of the nation they serve.

But let me not be misunderstood, there is all the difference between the attempt to debauch the subjects of a sovereign prince in order to ensnare them in conspiracy against him, and the legitimate endeavour to use every opportunity for acquiring information. The latter practice has always been permissible, and indeed is a necessary part of diplomacy. No criticism can fall upon a foreign envoy who successfully adopts the practice; the only culprit in such a case is the citizen of a foreign state who from corrupt motives sells information

Secret Service No Abuse of Immunity.

abroad. Apart from considerations of international law the interest of the public peace demands the preservation of the privileges of foreign envoys, for otherwise wars would be even more frequent than they are, because no prince would permit insults to his ministers to go unavenged. They are rightly resented, and the prince may pay heavily in his own peace of mind and the repose of his subjects for a moment of passion. He need do no more, however, than demand satisfaction for the bad conduct of any foreign envoy, and if he has just cause of complaint he will probably receive it. In any case the dismissal or recall of an ambassador will be read as a pointed lesson to all his colleagues in diplomacy, who will then understand that the price of evil conduct is the humiliation of dismissal.

The Credentials of an Ambassador. When an ambassador is sent to a foreign court, his master gives him a letter addressed to the foreign prince requesting him to give the same credence to the bearer of the letter as to its writer. This despatch is called a letter of credence, which thus establishes the identity of its bearer and stands as the hall-mark of his office. In France there are two sorts of letters of credence : one called *Lettre de Cachet*, which is despatched and countersigned by the Secretary of State for Foreign Affairs, and sometimes also called *Lettre de la Chancellerie*. The

other is written by the hand of one of the royal
private secretaries, and signed by the King himself ;
it is countersigned by any minister, and is usually
handed direct in private audience to the foreign
prince to whom it is addressed. The former type
of letter is presented in ceremonial public audience.
When a negotiator is appointed by his prince to a
free state or an assembly, which for this purpose is
treated as though it were a court, he does not receive
letters of credence, but his character and identity
are fully established in his full powers, which he
must exchange with ministers on arriving. The
document known as full powers is an authorisation
by the prince to his representative abroad to undertake all kinds of public business, the results of which
the sovereign himself agrees to accept by the proxy
of his minister ; but as a rule in such full powers
the particular matter under discussion is carefully specified, and the authority to act is confined
to it.

There are two kinds of full powers : one deriving *Full Powers.*
directly from the sovereign and the other from his
deputies, that is to say, his ministers of state who
have sufficient authority to nominate plenipoten-
tiaries in his absence. Such powers are particularly
desirable where the states lie far apart from one
another. In such negotiations as those between
the Court of Madrid and the Low Countries, or the

different Italian states, the advantage of this procedure is obvious. . . . Passports are of course merely letters which establish the identity and good faith of the person as distinct from the representative of state, and they are given even in time of war in order to secure a safe passage between countries at war for ministers engaged upon negotiation which may lead to peace. . . .

Instructions. The instruction is a written document containing a statement of the principal intentions of the prince or the state ; it is to be regarded as a general aid to memory and a general guide to conduct. It is secret and must be retained under the control of him who receives it, though of course there are occasions on which he will receive the command to communicate specific portions of it to a foreign minister or a foreign prince. Such communication is regarded as a rule as a mark of special confidence, but on the other hand it often happens that two instructions are given, one the ostensible, that is to say it is drawn up in such terms that it can be shown to other princes, and the other secret, which contains the true and final intentions of the prince himself. But even the latter type of instruction is subject to alteration by the daily despatches which the negotiator receives from home, and which ought to be read as so many new instructions drawn up in accordance with the reports which he has transmitted to his own court. It follows therefore that the manner of reports which a negotiator despatches to his home government will have a large influence upon the type of instruction which he receives from time to time.

The Minister of Foreign Affairs may prefer not *Oral* to put the instructions and intentions of his royal *Instructions.* master into writing but to deliver them orally, because then he has a greater freedom of interpretation according to circumstances as they arise, than he would have if he were bound by the written word. There is further a danger that such instructions when committed to paper may be wittingly or unwittingly left in the hands of some foreign diplomatist belonging to the opposite party. The risks thus incurred are too obvious to need any emphasis of mine. Whereas if the instructions be left in oral form, they can at least be repudiated if a dangerous situation were to arise from their being made known to an enemy prince. There are of course occasions where it is impossible not to commit to writing instructions given to a plenipotentiary, but it is a good rule in all negotiation to delay the issue of formal and binding instructions to as late a date in the negotiations as possible, so that the general lines upon which it is likely to proceed may be present to the mind of the minister who draws them up for the guidance of the ambassador.

It is not permissible without a serious violation of the law of nations to compel a minister to show his instructions in order to prove his good faith, nor is it permissible for a minister to communicate it in any form without an express command from his master, for he can fully rely on his letter of credence to establish both his identity and his good faith; besides which he is equipped with full powers in which the business of his negotiation is always fully described.

Discretionary Freedom.

Now such instructions may be as judicious and astute as can be imagined, but their use will lie in the wise interpretation by the diplomatist himself; and, as I have pointed out, the really able negotiator will always know how best to execute his master's commands so that the instructions received from him may be drawn up on information which is both up-to-date and adequate. Thus it is that while the final responsibility for all success or failure in diplomacy would seem to rest upon the King and his ministers at home, it is none the less true that since these ministers can only act upon information from abroad, the influence which an enlightened diplomatist can exercise upon the actions and designs of the home government is very large. Incapable men acting abroad will make nothing even of the most brilliant instructions; capable men by the accuracy and sagacity of their reports and suggestions can do much to improve even the most mediocre instructions, and therefore the responsibility for diplomatic action is in reality shared in about equal degree between the home government and its servants abroad. The home government cannot know when the opportunity for appropriate action will arise, and therefore the reports on foreign situations which are transmitted in despatches from diplomats abroad ought to be so designed as to present as far as possible an intelligent description of events.

What an astonishing diversity and inequality *Value of the* there is in the conduct of men. No one, not even *Trained Mind.* a minister of state, would think of building a house without the assistance of the best architect and the best workmen whom he could find; but it is the commonest occurrence to find that those who are charged with the transaction of very important state business, upon which the weal or woe of the whole realm depends, never think of entrusting it to trained minds, but give it to the first comer, whether he be a cunning architect or a mere hewer of stone. Therefore ministers and other persons in authority are culpable in a high degree if they do not secure for the foreign service of the state the most capable and sagacious men. For the errors in diplomacy sometimes bring more calamitous results than mistakes in other walks of life, and unless the negotiator can intelligently discern the coming event, he may plunge himself, his master, and his native land in irretrievable disaster.

Incompetence the Parent of Disaster. It is a crime against the public safety not to uproot incapacity wherever it is discovered, or to allow an incompetent diplomatist to remain one moment longer than necessary in a place where competency is sorely needed. Faults in domestic policy are often more easily remedied than mistakes in foreign policy. There are many factors in foreign affairs which lie beyond the control of the ministers of any given state, and all foreign action requires greater circumspection, greater knowledge, and far greater sagacity than is demanded in home affairs. Therefore the government cannot exercise too great a care in its choice of men to serve abroad. In making such a choice the Foreign Minister must set his face like a flint against all family influence and private pressure, for nepotism is the damnation of diplomacy. He is in some sense the guarantor to his Majesty of those whom he presents as diplomatists. Their good success will do him honour, their failure will fall with redoubled force upon his head, and may require herculean efforts by him in order to repair the damage it has caused. Hence it is of the first interest, both for the Foreign Minister himself and for the well-being of the state, to see that the high

94

public offices of diplomacy are not filled by the intrigues and personal cabals which reign at every court, and which often place in the King's hands unworthy instruments of his policy.

Now when a diplomatist has been appointed to a foreign post his first care should be to ask for the despatches of his predecessor in order that he may inform himself exactly of the state of affairs with which he will have to deal. *The Diplomatist prepares Himself for a Foreign Mission.* He will thus be able to pick up the thread and to make use both of the knowledge and of the different personal relationships which have gathered round the embassy during his predecessor's term of office. And as all public affairs are like a great network, one linked with another, it is of the first importance that a diplomatist proceeding to a foreign post should be a complete master of recent history both in regard to his own state and in regard to the relations which exist between the country of his new service and all neighbouring countries. Therefore, when the newly appointed diplomatist has read with care the despatches of his predecessor, he should make notes upon them, endeavouring to foresee the difficulties which he will meet both in such trivial matters as a novel ceremonial, or in the more weighty business of state, so that he may be able to discuss them with his own Foreign Minister, and thus receive what enlightenment he can.

He must study his own Foreign Office. Now, no matter how far-seeing a minister may be, it is impossible for him to foresee everything or to give such ample and at the same time precise instructions to his negotiators as to guide them in all circumstances which may arise. It is therefore of the first importance that the newly appointed diplomatist travelling to a far country should devote all his time before his departure to the discovery of the real intentions and designs of his own Foreign Office. In a word, he should saturate his mind with the thoughts of his master. He should not only consult those who have discharged diplomatic duties at the foreign court to which he is about to proceed, but should make it his especial care to keep touch with those who have lived in the country in any quality whatsoever, and to acquire from them all the knowledge which they may possess. Even the humblest of such persons may be able to give him information which will help him to regulate his conduct abroad. And before his departure he should certainly strike up an acquaintance with the ambassador representing the country to which he is about to proceed, in order that he may get from him private letters of recommendation, and further, in order that he may persuade him of his own earnest desire to do all in his power to establish good relations between the two states. He should let it be known to the foreign ambassador in question that he will lose no opportunity of bearing witness to the success of his mission and to the esteem which he has won at home. In so doing he will be able rapidly to acquire new and powerful friends in his new sphere of labour. For it is a commonplace of human experience that men will do as they are done by : reciprocity is the surest foundation of friendship.

The careful diplomatist will pay the same atten- *Choice of a* tion to the choice of his domestics as to more im- *Staff.* portant subjects. Those about him must do him credit. A well-ordered household served by reliable and well-mannered persons is a good advertisement, both of the ambassador and of the country whence he comes, and in order that they may have no excuse for ill-regulated conduct, he should set a high example before them in his own person. His choice of a private secretary is perhaps the most important of all, for if he be light-headed, frivolous or indiscreet, he may do his master irreparable harm ; and if he be a person liable to get into debt, his embarrassment may be the cause of very serious trouble. Some years ago the private secretary of a French ambassador sold the private cipher of the embassy for a large sum in order to wipe out his debts. Thus the ambassador's despatches were intercepted and read, with very grave results upon the relations between the two countries, in spite of

the fact that the obvious interest of both lay in the
same direction. The necessity for having faithful
and able men as secretaries has given rise to the belief that it would be very useful to establish them
in rank as a part of the public service of the King,
and thus to restore a custom which was abolished
some time ago in France. It would be a desirable
practice, for thereby a large body of men might
be trained in the diplomatic service of the Crown
from whom ambassadors and envoys could be
drawn. This is the practice in several foreign
countries, and there is no doubt that it leads to
the improvement of the whole diplomatic service.
For if the secretaries and attachés are selected and
paid by the King's government they will tend to
acquire a careful efficiency and *esprit de corps* which
will be the best protection for his secrets. And it
is obvious that as long as the choice of such persons
is left to the personal decision of the ambassador
alone there is always a risk that he will not be able
to offer a sufficient sum to command the services of
good men. Thus the adequate payment and proper
official recognition of such junior diplomatists is
a necessary part of any true reform of the foreign
service, and it would certainly be a great relief to
most ambassadors to take the responsibility of choice
off their shoulders as well as the burden of paying
secretaries for their services. The state will cer-

tainly be well repaid if such a policy as I suggest be adopted, for diplomacy will then become the school in which good workmen will rapidly learn the use of their tools.

On arrival at a foreign court a negotiator should *First Steps at the Foreign Court.* make himself and his mission known to the proper authorities at the earliest possible moment, and request a private audience with the prince in order that he may establish contact immediately, and thus prepare the way for good relations between his master and the foreign sovereign. When he has taken the necessary steps for this purpose he should be in no hurry to embark upon any important steps but should rather study the *terrain.* For this purpose he should remain a watchful, silent observer of the habits of the court and of the government, and if he be in a country where the prince is really the ruler, he should study with the greatest assiduity the whole life and habits of the latter ; for policy is not merely a matter of high impersonal design, it is a vast complexity in which the inclinations, the judgments, the virtues and the vices of the prince himself will play a large part. Occasions will constantly arise in which the adroit negotiator who has equipped himself with this knowledge will be able to use it with the highest possible effect. And he should test his own conclusions by comparing notes dis-

99

creetly with other foreign negotiators of the same court, especially if they have had a long residence there. Up to a certain point co-operation between foreign ambassadors is not only permissible but desirable and necessary. And since no prince, not even the most autocratic, discharges the duties of government entirely by himself without confiding in one or more favoured ministers, the negotiator should make it his business to know much of the ministers and confidants surrounding the King who have his fullest confidence, for in the same manner as described above personal qualities, opinions, passions, likes, and dislikes are all relevant subjects of study, and should be carefully observed by every negotiator who means business.

Relations with Colleagues. When a foreign envoy arrives at a court and has been received by the prince, he should inform all the other members of the Corps Diplomatique either by a squire of his suite or by a secretary. They will then pay him their first visit, but he will receive no visits until he has gone through the formality of announcing to each in turn his own arrival; and at a court where there are ambassadors of several kings, each on arrival should pay his respects first of all to the French ambassador, who everywhere takes first rank. The Spaniards, who adopted every form of chicane for a whole century in order to avoid the recognition of French precedence,

which for that matter is an immemorial right of
the French King, finally recognised it by the public
declaration, made by Philip IV. to his Majesty in
1662 by the Marquis de la Fuente, the Spanish
ambassador in Paris, which arose out of the violent
dispute in London between the Count d'Estrade
and the Baron de Vatville, after which no Spanish
ambassador would consent to be present at any
ceremony attended by the French ambassador.
Various other attempts have been made to dispute
French supremacy, but with no result. . . .

After he has fully informed himself of all such *Report of First*
matters and placed himself in such a position as to *Impressions.*
know immediately whether the prince has changed
his mind or tranferred his confidence from one
servant to another, he should set all these things
down faithfully in a despatch to his home government, presenting a full picture of the court as he
sees it, and at the same time setting down the conclusions which he has drawn from his observations.
He should not fail to indicate the methods by which
he proposes to act, or the means he proposes to use,
in order to carry out the commands which he has
received. At the same time he will not fail to keep
his own knowledge up to date, and to use it for
finding and keeping open every possible avenue of
approach to the prince to whom he is accredited,
or to his ministers and favourites. There is no

doubt that the surest and best way in which the negotiator can establish good relations is to prove to both courts that their union is of great mutual advantage. It is the essential design of diplomacy to confer such a mutual advantage, and to carry policy to success by securing the co-operation in it of those who might otherwise be its opponents. Success won by force or by fraud stands upon a weak foundation. Diplomatic success, on the other hand, won by methods which confer reciprocal benefits on both parties, must be regarded not only as firmly founded, but as the sure promise of other successes to come. I am not so foolish as to suppose, however, that this method can be applied in every situation. There are times when it is necessary for the negotiator to exploit the hatreds, passions, and jealousies of those with whom he deals, and therefore occasion will arise when it is easier and more fruitful to appeal to prejudice rather than to any estimate of the true and permanent interests of those concerned. As we have observed above, both kings and nations often plunge into reckless courses of policy under the impulse of passion, and as a rule throw overboard all consideration of their veritable interests.

Character and Whims of the Foreign Prince. The high elevation of crowned heads does not prevent them from being human ; and indeed in some ways it lays them open to certain weaknesses of which lesser men by reason of their position are largely free. There is a certain pride of position, a certain arrogant self-esteem, which is only to be found in highly placed persons, and which is most marked in kings and ministers. On this account, and on account of the actual power their exalted position puts into their hands, kings are open to persuasion and flattery in a way in which men of lower degree cannot be approached. This consideration must ever be in the mind of the good negotiator, who should therefore strive to divest himself of his own feelings and prejudices, and place himself in the position of the King so that he may understand completely the desires and whims which guide his actions. And when he has done so he should say to himself : ' Now, if I were in the place of this prince, wielding his power, subject to his passions and prejudices, what effect would my mission and my arguments have upon me ? ' The more often he thus puts himself in the position of others, the more subtle and effective will his arguments be. And it is of course not only in matters of opinion that this use of the imagination is valuable, it is more particularly in all those personal aspects where the power to give pleasure by flattery or any other means is effective.

No one will forget that crowned heads, and even *The Use of* their ministers themselves, are accustomed from *Compliments.*

birth to the submission of those around them, to receive their respect and praise. This unbroken experience of the obedience of others is apt to make them very sensitive to criticism, and unwilling to listen to contradiction. There are few princes to whom it is easy to speak the truth, and since it is not part of the business of the negotiator except on rare occasions to speak home truths at a foreign court, he will avoid as far as possible everything which may wound the royal pride which is the natural result of the manner in which princes are reared. On the other hand, he will never give empty praise nor applaud a reprehensible act, and where praise is given as it is deserved, the negotiator must know how to clothe it in chaste and dignified language. And since princes are accustomed to hear their praise sung constantly, they become connoisseurs in praise and good judges of a timely compliment. It is the higher art of the subtle courtier to know how to deliver a well-turned compliment to his King, and above all, if the King is endowed with real intelligence, never to praise him for qualities which he does not possess. Any fool can earn the esteem of a prince who is also a fool by indiscriminate praise. Wise men will rely on their own merits and on the good sense of the King wherever they have the good fortune to serve a monarch so endowed. To praise a King for those things which are inherent in his position, such as riches, spacious mansions, and fine clothes, is merely stupidity. A King who is worth praising will only value your praise if it is given to qualities which he knows to be praiseworthy. In this matter the negotiator must be sufficiently worldly-wise always to remember that the good favour of the ladies of the court is to be won by different means than that of his Majesty or the ministers. And since, as I have pointed out elsewhere, the approach to the King and his ministers may perhaps be most easily made through feminine influence, the negotiator will study carefully the character and weaknesses of all the ladies at the court so as to keep these useful and attractive avenues open for his use.

The methods of giving pleasure, as I say, must vary. One of the most illustrious and sagacious *Craft at the Card Table.* ambassadors of our time, a friend of my own, neglected nothing, but he used to say that there was no surer road to the good-will of a sovereign than to allow him to win at the card-table, and that many a great enterprise had been conducted to success by the little pile of gold coins which passed from him to his royal opponent at the gaming-table. My friend used to say in jest that he had played the fool at foreign card-tables in order to prove that he was a wise man at home ! His jest bore a truth within it which I hope every negotiator will lay to heart. . . .

The pleas which I have set out above are, I believe, applicable in most situations, but of course there are variations to be observed. It is not always easy for a negotiator on leaving home to remember how great a difference there is between his own court and that to which he proceeds. For whether the foreign country which is his new home stands on equal terms with his own or whether it be a Power of lower station in the world, the vast differences in national outlook between them must be fully understood before the negotiator can make any progress. It is therefore his first business, whatever be the magnitude and splendour of the court to which he is accredited, to win the general favour by showing a genuine and sincere interest in the welfare of his new associates, and in all the customs of the court and the habits of the people ; and on his arrival he should show himself ready to share information both with his new colleagues in the Corps Diplomatique, and with the ministers of the King to whom he is sent. Let me lay some insistence on this. It will be observed that if a negotiator has the reputation of speaking freely on many subjects, it is not improbable that those who have secrets to reveal may speak the more freely to him. A negotiator of my acquaintance to

NEGOTIATING WITH PRINCES

whom I look with high regard once said : ' Diplomacy is like a chain of ten links in which perhaps
only one is missing to make it complete : it is the
business of the diplomat to supply the tenth link.'
This is true, and I believe that the diplomatist who
is least enwrapped in secrecy will most quickly and
surely discover it.   It is therefore important that
the negotiator, being well equipped with all kinds
of information, should be guided by a sound judgment in the use of it.   He should realise that in all
information there are only one or two items which
are of the first importance, and that therefore the
freedom with which he uses the rest need not in
any way imperil his master's plans.   The more
freely he can share such information, and the more
carefully he bestows his praise upon individuals,
the more surely will men say of him that he is a
reliable person, and will turn to him in moments
of crisis.

Every right-minded man desires to stand well in *The Clock-*
the eyes of those with whom he transacts business, *maker's*
and therefore he will give some trouble to all those *Patience.*
devices for securing the good-will of men to which
I have referred.   If he finds in the course of his
work that the prince himself or any one of his
ministers is ill-disposed towards him or intractable
in discussion, he must not on that account allow
himself to imitate the fault, but must redouble his

efforts in the contrary direction. Indeed he must behave as a good watchmaker would when his clock has gone out of order : he must labour to remove the difficulty, or at all events to circumvent its results. He must not be led aside by his own feelings. Prejudice is a great misinterpreter's house in all public affairs.

A High Ideal. It might seem that the ideal which I now set up for the negotiator is one too high for any man to reach. It is true that no man can ever carry out his instructions without a fault, but unless he has before him an ideal as a guide he will find himself plunged in the midst of distracting affairs without any rule for his own conduct. Therefore I place before him these considerations : that despite all disappointments and exasperations he must act with *sang-froid* ; he must work with patience to remove all obstacles that lie in his path, whether they are placed there by accident or act of God or by the evil design of men ; he must preserve a calm and resolute mind when the conjunctures of events seem to conspire against him ; and finally, he must remember that if once he permit his own personal or outrageous feelings to guide his conduct in negotiation he is on the sure and straight road to disaster. In a word, when events and men are unkind he must never despair of being able to change them, nor again when they smile upon his efforts must he cherish the illusion that their good favour will endure for ever.

The functions of a minister despatched on a *The Negoti-* mission to a foreign country fall into two principal *ator's Two-* *fold Function.* categories : the first to conduct the business of his master, and the second to discover the business of others. The first of these concerns the prince or his ministers of state, or at all events those deputies to whom are entrusted the examination of his proposals. In all these different kinds of negotiation he must seek success principally by his straightforward and honest procedure, for if he attempts to succeed by subtlety or by a sense of superiority over those with whom he is engaged he may very likely deceive himself. There is no prince or state which does not possess some shrewd envoy to discern its real interests. And indeed, even among people who seem to be the least refined, there are often those who know their own interests best, and follow them with the most constancy. Therefore the negotiator, no matter how able he may be, must not attempt to teach such persons their own business, but he should exhaust all the resources of his mind and wit to prove to them the great advantage of the proposals which he has to make.

An ancient philosopher once said that friendship between men is nothing but a commerce in which

*Diplomacy a
Commerce in
Benefits.*

each seeks his own interest. The same is true or even truer of the liaisons and treaties which bind one sovereign to another, for there is no durable treaty which is not founded on reciprocal advantage, and indeed a treaty which does not satisfy this condition is no treaty at all, and is apt to contain the seeds of its own dissolution. Thus the great secret of negotiation is to bring out prominently the common advantage to both parties of any proposal, and so to link these advantages that they may appear equally balanced to both parties. For this purpose when negotiations are on foot between two sovereigns, one the greater and the other the less, the more powerful of these two should make the first advance, and even undertake a large outlay of money to bring about the union of interests with his lesser neighbour, for his own self-interest will show him that he has really the greater object and the larger advantages in view, and that any benefits he may confer or subsidies which he may grant to his weaker ally will be readily repaid by the success of his designs. Now, as we have said, the secret of negotiation is to harmonise the interests of the parties concerned. It is clear that if a negotiator excludes the honest and straightforward method of reason and persuasion, and adopts on the contrary a haughty and menacing manner, then obviously he must be followed by an army ready to invade the country in which he has put forth such provocative claims. Without such a display of force his claims will fall to the ground, even though by advantageous arguments they might have prevailed with the prince whom he addressed, and who might have accepted them had they been proposed in a different manner. When a prince or a state is powerful enough to dictate to his neighbours the art of negotiation loses its value, for then there is need for nothing but a mere statement of the prince's will ; but when there is a balance of force an independent prince will only decide to favour one of the two parties of a dispute if he discerns advantages to himself and good results to the prosperity of his realm.

A prince who has no powerful enemies can easily *Harmony the* impose tribute on all neighbouring Powers, but a *Ideal State.* prince whose aim is self-aggrandisement and who has powerful enemies must seek allies among the lesser states in order to increase those friendly to him ; and if possible he should be able to prove his power by the benefits which an alliance with him can confer upon them. Therefore the principal function of the negotiator is to bring about a harmonised union between his master and the sovereign to whom he is sent, or else to maintain and increase existing alliances by every means in his power. He must labour to remove misunderstandings, to prevent subjects of dispute from arising, and generally to maintain in that foreign country the honour and interests of his prince. This includes the protection and patronage of his subjects, assistance to their business enterprises, and the promotion of good relations between them and the subjects of the foreign prince to whose court he is accredited. He must always assume that there is no prince nor state in the world which does not desire to avoid a condition of crisis, and that those princes who love to fish in troubled waters will never lack the means to stir them up, but that the storms which such men conjure up are apt to overwhelm them, so that the wise negotiator will do all he can to avoid giving provocation, and will conduct himself in such a manner that no one will be able to impute reckless motives to him.

The Search for Information.

His second function being the discovery of all that is happening at court and in the cabinet, he should first of all take steps to learn from his predecessor all that he knows regarding the state of affairs in the country to which he is about to proceed and to acquire from him those hints and suggestions which may be of use. He should take up the friends and acquaintances left behind by his predecessor, and should add to them by making new ones. It would be no bad practice in this matter to imitate the established rule of the Venetian

NEGOTIATING WITH PRINCES

Republic, which obliges an ambassador returning from a foreign court to render a detailed account in writing of the country, both for the information of the public and for the instruction of his successor at the embassy. The diplomatists of Venice have drawn great advantage from this practice, and it has been often remarked that there are no better instructed negotiators in Europe than those of Venice.

The discovery of the course of events and the trend of policy in a foreign country is most natural *Freemasonry of Diplomacy.* when one knows both the personnel and the political habits of the country, and a negotiator for the first time in such a country must neglect no source of information. In addition to those mentioned above, he may very probably find that his colleagues in the Corps Diplomatique will be of use to him, for since the whole diplomatic body works for the same end, namely to discover what is happening, there may arise—there often indeed does arise—a freemasonry of diplomacy by which one colleague informs another of coming events which a lucky chance has enabled him to discern. Such collaboration is possible in all cases except those in which their sovereigns are at variance. As regards the information which can be drawn from the people of the country itself, the surest and shortest method is to make a confidant of some one already in the counsels of the foreign prince, but this must be done only by such means as will enable the negotiator to keep a check upon his correspondent, and thus prevent any damage to his master's plans. This action is very necessary, for in diplomacy as in war there are such things as double spies paid by both parties. The cleverest of these will begin by giving true information and good advice in order the more thoroughly to deceive the negotiator at a later date. There have even been princes subtle enough to see the advantage of permitting their confidants to behave thus, and I know of cases where the confidant of a sovereign, under the appearance of a secret liaison with a foreign envoy, gave the latter true and false information at the same time, and thus effectively masked the designs of his master. An ambassador must always be on his guard against such deception.

The Foolish Dutchman. There was in England in 1671 a Dutch ambassador who was so easily persuaded by certain privy counsellors of King Charles II. that their master had no intention to go to war with the States General that in his despatches home he gave the most explicit assurance that there was nothing to fear from England, treating with ridicule the opinion that London had resolved to attack them; and we have since learned that these English counsellors had been deliberately detailed by the King to play upon the

114

credulity of the Dutch ambassador. There have been in our time ambassadors of other countries who have done the same.

Now the astute negotiator will not likely believe *All News must* everything he hears, nor accept advice which he *be tested.* cannot test; he must examine the origin of information, as well as the interest and the motives of those who offer it him. He must attempt to discover the means by which they themselves have acquired it, and he must compare it with other information to see whether it tallies with that part which he knows to be true. There are many signs by which a discerning and penetrating mind will be able to read the truth by placing each link of information in contact with another. For this purpose no rules can be drawn up for the guidance of a diplomat in such a matter, for unless a man be born with such qualities he cannot acquire them, and to those who do not possess them I might as well speak to the deaf as write these observations.

A negotiator can discover national secrets by *The Flair for* frequenting the company of those in authority, and *Secrets.* there is not a court in the world where ministers or others are not open to various kinds of approach, either because they are indiscreet and often say more than they should, or because they are discontented and ready to reveal secrets in order to satisfy their jealousy. And even the most practised and reliable ministers are not always on their guard. I have seen highly trained and well-proven statesmen who none the less in the course of conversation, and by other signs, allowed expressions to escape them which gave important clues to their policy. And there are courtiers at every court who, though not members of the King's Council, know by long practice how to discover a secret, and who are always prepared to reveal it in order to show their own importance and their penetration. It is almost impossible to conceal from an active, observant, and enlightened negotiator any important design of public policy, for no departure of state can ever be made without great preparation which entails the sharing of many secrets by many persons, and this is a danger against which it is almost impossible to guard even by those who take the greatest precautions.

On the Transmission of Information. Now in the transmission of information of this kind the negotiator must give an exact account of all the circumstances surrounding it, that is to say, how and by whom he acquired it; and he should accompany it with his own comments and conjectures in order that the prince may be fully informed, and may be able to judge whether the conclusions drawn from all the circumstances are well or ill founded. There are certain things which a clever minister will discover for himself, and of which he must give an exact account to his master, for such knowledge is often a sure clue even to the most secret designs. Thus he can by his own observation discover the passions and ruling interests of the prince to whose court he is sent : whether he is ambitious, painstaking, or observant ; whether he is warlike or prefers peace; whether he is the real ruler of the country, and if not by whom he is ruled; and in general what are the principal inclinations and the interests of those who have most influence over him. He must also inform himself exactly of the state of the military forces both on land and sea, of the number and strength of fortified places, whether they are always kept in a high state of efficiency and well supplied with ammunition, of the condition of the sea-ports, of his vessels of war, and of his arsenals, of the number of troops which he can put into the field at once, both of cavalry and of infantry, without stripping his fortresses bare of their garrisons. He must know the state of public opinion, whether it is well disposed or discontented ; he must keep in his hands the threads of every great intrigue, knowing all the factions and parties into which opinion is divided ; he must know the leanings of ministers and other persons in authority in such matters as religion. He should not even neglect the observation of the King's personal household, of the manner in which his domestic affairs are conducted, of his outlay, both on his household and on his military establishments, of the time spent in them, etc. He must know the alliances, both offensive and defensive, concluded with other Powers, especially those which appear hostile in design; he must be able to describe at any moment the attitude of all the principal states towards the court to which he is accredited, and to give an account of the diplomatic relations which exist between them.

Action Appropriate to Democratic States.

He must pay the prince assiduous attention, and thus acquire a sufficient familiarity with him to be able to see and speak to him frequently without ceremony, so that he may be always in a position to know what is going on, and to insinuate into the prince's mind what is favourable to his master's design. If he lives in a democratic state he must attend the Diet and other popular assemblies. He must keep open house and a well-garnished table to attract the deputies, and thus both by his honesty and by his presence gain the ear of the ablest and most authoritative politicians, who may be able to defeat a hostile design or support a favourable one. If people of this kind have a freedom of *entrée* to the ambassador, a good table will greatly assist in the discovery of all that is going on, and the expense laid out upon it is not merely honourable but extraordinarily useful if only the negotiator himself knows how to profit from it.

Indeed it is in the nature of things that good *The Value of* cheer is a great conciliator, that it fosters familiarity, *Good Cheer.* and promotes a freedom of exchange between the guests, while the warmth of wine will often lead to the discovery of important secrets. There are several other functions for the employment of public ministers, as for instance that of informing a prince of good or evil tidings regarding his own master, or that of conveying compliments or condolences in a similar case to the prince himself. A negotiator who knows his business will not neglect even the least of such opportunities, and he will perform his function in such a manner as to show that his master is truly interested in all that passes at the foreign court. Indeed the best negotiator is he who forestalls even the orders of his own master, and shows himself so apt a negotiator of his intentions that he is able to act in advance of each event of the kind, and thus present his master's sentiments in appropriate language before any other foreign diplomatist has even begun to consider the matter. And when he actually receives his master's orders on the subject, should they turn out to be of a somewhat different character than the expressions he has already used, his own adroit-

119

ness will enable him to bridge the apparent difference. The diplomatist's functions cease automatically on the death of his master or on the death of the prince to whom he is accredited, and are not revived until new letters of credence are received. They also come to an end on his withdrawal or upon a declaration of war, but it should be noted that the privileges attached to the office of ambassador under the law of nations continue unbroken, notwithstanding any declaration of war or other interpretation of his functions, and these privileges remain in force until he reaches his own national territory.

The Conduct of Negotiations. Diplomacy is a matter for orally conducted and for written communications. The first is the common method where one is dealing with a royal court, the second is usual in republics and those states in which assemblies, such as the Diet of the Empire of Switzerland, are the repositories of power. It is always the custom where states are assembled in France to exchange statements of policy in writing. But it is always more advantageous for the practised diplomatist to negotiate face to face, because by that means he can discover the true intentions of those with whom he is dealing. His own skill will then enable him both to act and to speak in an appropriate and apt fashion. Most men in handling public affairs pay more attention

120

to what they themselves say than to what is said to them.   Their minds are so full of their own notions that they can think of nothing but of obtaining the ears of others for them, and will hardly be prevailed on to listen to the statements of other people. This fault is peculiar to those lively and impatient nations like ours, who find it difficult to bridle impetuous temperaments.   It has often been noticed that in ordinary conversation Frenchmen speak all at one time, and interrupt one another incessantly, without attempting to hear what each has to say.

One of the most necessary qualities in a good *The Apt* negotiator is to be an apt listener ; to find a skilful *Listener.* yet trivial reply to all questions put to him, and to be in no hurry to declare either his own policy, still less his own feelings ; and on opening negotiations he should be careful not to reveal the full extent of his design except in so far as it is necessary to explore the ground ; and he should govern his own conduct as much by what he observes in the faces of others as by what he hears from their lips.   One of the great secrets of diplomacy is to sift the real from the trivial, and so to speak, to distil drop by drop into the minds of your competitors those causes and arguments which you wish them to adopt.   By this means your influence will spread gradually through their minds almost unawares. In acting thus the negotiator will bear in mind that the majority of men will never enter upon a vast undertaking, even though advantageous to themselves, without they can see beforehand the whole length of the journey upon which they are asked to embark. Its magnitude will deter them. But if they can be brought to take successfully one step after another they will find themselves at the end of the journey almost unawares. Herein is to be found the importance of not revealing vast designs except to a few chosen spirits whose minds are properly attuned to them.

Diplomacy a Bowling Green.

A truth of this kind applies to friend and foe alike. Thus in the approach to difficult negotiations the true dexterity of diplomacy, like a good bowler using the run of the green, consists in finding the existing bias of the matter. As Epictetus, the ancient philosopher, said in his manual : ' There are in every matter two handles, the one by which it is easy to carry, the other difficult. Do not take it by the difficult end, for if you do so you will neither be able to lift it nor carry it. But if you take it by the right side you will carry it without trouble.' Now the easiest way to find the right bias is to make each proposition which you put forward appear as a statement of the interests of those with whom you are negotiating, for since diplomacy is the attempt to find a basis of common action or agreement, it is obvious that the more the opposing party can be brought to see your designs in their own light and to accept them thus, the more surely will their co-operation for any action be fruitful alike to themselves and to you.

Now, of course there are few men who will en-tirely divest themselves of their own sentiments in favour of those of others, or who will confess that they were wrong, especially if the matter be conducted in an acrimonious discussion in which the negotiator meets all arguments freely by contradiction. But none the less the astute diplomatist will know how to exploit human nature in such a manner as to cause even the most stiff-necked opponents gradually to relax their hold upon certain opinions ; and this may be most easily attained by abandoning the approach which caused the original dispute, and taking up the matter from another aspect. Thus by flattery of his *amour-propre*, or by some other device which may put him in a good humour, the competitor in a negotiation may be brought to consider the matter in a new light, and to accept at the end of the negotiation that which he repudiated with violence at its commencement. And, however unreasonable the majority of mankind is, it will always be observed that men retain so much respect for reason that they will always hope to be judged by the other man as acting

The Bias of Human Nature.

upon reasonable grounds. The negotiator will
know how to exploit this subtle form of intellectual
pride. And especially where there is more than
one party to the negotiation the astute diplomatist
will be able to exploit the foibles of each of the
other two parties, and yet to flatter each in turn
for his reasonable and statesmanlike attitude.

Ce n'est que le premier pas qui coûte. Above all, at the commencement of a negotiation,
as I have said, it is necessary in any long and
complicated business to present the matter in hand
in its easiest and most advantageous light, and so to
speak to insinuate all parties into it so that they
may be well launched upon the whole enterprise
before they are aware of its magnitude. For this
purpose the negotiator must appear as an agreeable,
enlightened, and far-seeing person ; he must beware
of trying to pass himself off too conspicuously as
a crafty or adroit manipulator. The essence of
skill lies in concealing it, and the negotiator must
ever strive to leave an impression upon his fellow
diplomatists of his sincerity and good faith. And
he should beware of attempting to force a decision,
or to ride roughshod over difficulties that are raised,
for if he behaves thus he will not fail to draw upon
himself the aversion of those with whom he is dealing, and thus to bring prejudice upon his master's
designs. It would be better for him to pass for
less enlightened than he really is, and he should

attempt to carry his own policy to success by good and solid reasons rather than by pouring contempt upon the policy of others. The opposite fault is equally to be avoided. The negotiator must not let himself pass under the influence of other men, especially of those powerful personalities whose wont it is to sway the minds of all whom they meet.

The more powerful the prince, the more suave *Diplomacy* should his diplomatist be, for since power of that *does not thrive* *upon Menaces.* kind is likely to awaken jealousy in his neighbours, the diplomat should let it speak for itself, and rather use his own powers of persuasion by means of moderation to support the just rights of his prince than to vaunt his power or the extent of his dominions. Menaces always do harm to negotiation, and they frequently push one party to extremities to which they would not have resorted without provocation. It is well known that injured vanity frequently drives men into courses which a sober estimate of their own interests would lead them to avoid. Of course when a prince has real subjects of complaint against another, especially against an inferior, in circumstances where it is necessary to make an example of the delinquent, the blow must fall immediately after the threat is given, so that the delinquent cannot be in a position, either by the delays of diplomacy or by any other means, to shield himself from just punishment. The longer the delay is between the threat and its fulfilment, the more likely it is that the culprit will be able to form alliances with other Powers, and thus avoid the just chastisement of the prince whom he has wronged.

The Good Christian.

The wise and enlightened negotiator must of course be a good Christian, and he must let his character appear in all his speeches, in his way of living, and must forbid evil and loose-living persons to cross his threshold. Justice and modesty should govern all his actions ; he should be respectful to princes ; affable and approachable with his equals ; considerate to his inferiors, and civil and honest with everybody.

At Home in the Foreign Country.

He must fall into the ways and customs of the country where he lives without showing repugnance or expressing contempt for them, as is frequently done by diplomatists who lose no opportunity of praising their own country and decrying all others. The diplomatist must bear in mind once for all that he is not authorised to demand that a whole nation shall conform to his way of living, and that it is more reasonable, and in the long run greatly to his own comfort, to accommodate himself to foreign ways of living. He should beware of criticising the form of government or the personal conduct of the prince to whom he is accredited. On the contrary he should always praise that which is praiseworthy without affectation and without flattery, and if he properly understands his own function he will quickly discover that there is no nation or state which has not many good points, excellent laws, charming customs as well as bad ones ; and he will quickly discover that it is easy to single out the good points, and that there is no profit to be had in denouncing the bad ones, for the very good reason that nothing the diplomatist can say or do will alter the domestic habits or laws of the country in which he lives. He should take a pride in knowing the history of the country, so that he may be able to give the prince pleasure by praising the great feats of his ancestors, as well as for his own benefit to interpret current events in the light of the historical movements of the past. When it becomes known that the negotiator possesses such knowledge and uses it aptly, his credit will certainly rise, and if he is adroit enough to turn his conversations at court to those subjects of which he is a master, he will find that his diplomatic task is greatly assisted, and that the pleasure he gives to those around him is amply repaid to him in the smoothness of negotiation.

The diplomatist must, however, bear constantly *The Secret of* in mind both at work and at play the aims which *Success.* he is supposed to be serving in the foreign country, and should subordinate his personal pleasure and

all his occupations to their pursuit. In this matter
the two chief aims which the able negotiator places
before himself are, as I have said, to conduct the
affairs of his master to a prosperous issue, and to
spare no pains to discover the designs of others.
And since the means to be employed in both cases
are the same, namely by acquiring the esteem,
friendship, and confidence of the prince himself and
of those in authority around him, there is no surer
way of employing them than by becoming person-
ally agreeable. It is marvellous how a *persona grata*
may contrive to uproot even the deepest suspicions
and wipe out the memory of the gravest insults.
If the diplomatist be looked upon with disfavour
at the court he is not a true servant of his master's
interests ; for one who is out of favour will not be
in a position to know what is going on, and will
therefore be but a poor guide to his home government in assisting them to frame their policy. The
responsibility for placing the wrong kind of diplomatist in a good position rests of course with the
minister who appoints him, but there are many
cases in which an ill-fitting appointment has been
redeemed by the dauntless assiduity and unfailing
courtesy of the diplomatist himself ; but since this
imposes an unnecessary strain upon the ambassador,
the Foreign Minister should ever have a care to
appoint suitable men to all foreign posts.

128

NEGOTIATING WITH PRINCES

I have already described those characteristics *Support from* which compose suitability; I will but add here that *Home.* no diplomatist can succeed in his foreign task unless he is well supported by his own government and given every opportunity to understand its policy. By this means he will be in a position to exploit every situation as far as may be to advantage, and he will also be able to deny false rumours set afloat by the enemy. This support from his home government implies a complimentary application on his part, for it is of the highest importance that he should keep himself apprised of all contemporary movements in his own country; that he should know intimately the personal character both of the sovereign and of his Foreign Minister, so that in moments of doubt he may be able to guess shrewdly what is in the mind of those who employ him. Without such knowledge he will certainly go astray, and without a constant contact with his home government the conduct of diplomacy cannot possibly prosper in his hands.

As regards the relations which the diplomatist *Good Faith the* maintains in a foreign country, we must observe *Best Weapon.* that while his success will partly depend upon his affability to all men, he must use the utmost discretion in all his more intimate relationships, and, above all, he should try to form professional friendships on the basis of mutual advantage and respect.

There is no permanence in a relationship begun by promises which cannot be redeemed, and therefore, as I have said before, the use of deceit in diplomacy is of necessity restricted, for there is no curse which comes quicker to roost than a lie which has been found out.   Beyond the fact that a lie is unworthy of a great minister, it actually does more harm than good to policy because, though it may confer success to-day, it will create an atmosphere of suspicion which will make success impossible to-morrow.   No doubt an ambassador will receive a great deal of information which it is his duty to transmit; but if he is not in a position to test it he will merely pass it on without comment or guarantee of its truth.   In general it should be the highest aim of the diplomatist to gain such a reputation for good faith with his own government and also abroad that they will place reliance both upon his information and upon the advice which he gives.

The Value of a Candid Report.   In this respect he should take good care in reporting the course of negotiations to his master from time to time not to hold out prospects of success before success itself is in his grasp.   It is much better that he should depict the difficulties of the case and the improbability of success even when he is virtually sure in his own mind that he will succeed.   He will acquire vastly greater credit by success in an undertaking of which he himself promises little than he will in one upon which he has reported favourably throughout. It is always good for the credit of a negotiator if good reports of him arrive from different sources, for such independent proof of the value of a diplomatist's services must be highly prized by every prince, and will redound to the benefit of the diplomatist himself. It is obvious that the more successful he is in the relationships which he forms at a foreign court, the more surely will the diplomatist receive such independent testimony to his merit. But let him not seek such testimony by unworthy means. For this purpose he should neither bribe the servants of others, nor take natives of a foreign court into his own service. It is too obvious that they will probably be spies.

He himself ought never to consent to accept gifts *On Accepting* from a foreign court except with the express know- *Gifts.* ledge and permission of his master, or in such cases as are commonly permitted by the usage of the court, such as those given on the arrival or departure of an ambassador. He who receives gifts on any other condition may be accused of selling himself, and therefore of betraying the prince whom he serves. Unless he preserves his independence he cannot possibly represent his own master or maintain the high dignity of his office. This dignity must be kept beyond suspicion. It is indispensable to every ambassador, though it need not be carried out at all times and at all places, for the diplomatist will readily understand that at certain times he can win the good grace of those around him by living in an easy, affable, and familiar manner among his friends. To wrap oneself in official dignity at all times is mere preposterous arrogance, and the diplomatist who behaves thus will repel rather than attract.

The Tale of Don Estevan de Gamarre. There are many important occasions when the diplomatist will require all his wit and all his prudence. It will often happen that he has to tell bad news or give unpalatable advice to a prince accustomed to be flattered by his ministers, who for various private reasons usually conceal bad news from him. Let me give an example of what I mean : Don Estevan de Gamarre had served the King of Spain for many years with zeal and fidelity both in war and in diplomacy, particularly in the Low Countries where he had been ambassador for a long time. He had a relative in the King's Council fully disposed to put the ambassador's services in the best light, and yet he received no reward, while late-comers of all kinds received advancement to high offices both at home and abroad. He resolved to go to Madrid to discover the cause of his evil fortune. He complained to his relative the minister, giving a number of instances in which important services which he had rendered had been passed over and forgotten., The minister having heard him, quietly replied that he had no one to blame but himself, and that if he had been as good a courtier as he was a brilliant diplomatist and faithful subject, he would have received the same advancement as those whose deserts were less, but that his sincerity was an obstacle to his good fortune, for his despatches were always full of distasteful truths which set the King's teeth on edge. For instance, when the French gained a victory he told the story faithfully and without regard for Spanish feelings in his despatches. Or if they set siege to a town, he would predict its certain fall unless help were sent. Or in another case, where an ally had expressed displeasure because the Spanish Court seemed likely not to keep faith with it, he insisted that the King should keep his word in language which was neither diplomatic nor persuasive, and all the while other Spanish negotiators in other parts of France, with better eye to their own interests, were informing the King that the French were decadent, that their armies were undisciplined and quite incapable of effective campaigning, and so on : to which the minister himself added that the King in Council could not too highly reward those who sent such good news, nor

The King's Teeth on Edge.

too readily forget a man like himself who never wrote anything but the unpalatable truth.

Deceit in Favour in Madrid. Thereupon Don Estevan de Gamarre, in his surprise at this picture of the Court of Spain drawn for him by his relative, replied : ' Apparently fortune in Madrid favours the deceiver and the favour of the Court may be won by mendacity. I have no longer any qualms about my future.' He then returned to the Low Countries, where he profited so easily by the advice of his relative, that, to employ a Spanish term, he won several *mercedes*, and he saw his own affairs prosper in the measure in which he succeeded in inventing reasons why the affairs of the enemy must come to nought. From this one may conclude that the Court of Spain wished to be deceived, and gave its ambassadors a free rein to make their own fortunes at the expense of the true interests of the monarchy. There is a moral here both for ministers at home and for ambassadors abroad, on which I need not insist. The truth requires two agents, one to tell and another to hear.

On Treaties and their Ratifications. Between sovereign states there are many kinds of treaty, the principal of which are treaties of peace, armistices, commercial treaties, and those which regulate alliances or guarantee neutrality. There are both public and secret treaties. There are even contingent treaties, so called because their success depends upon future events. When the ministers of two equal Powers sign a treaty they make two copies of it which are called a double instrument. In each copy the ambassador who draws it up places the name of his own prince at the head and signs his in order at the foot, thereby indicating that neither he nor his master relinquishes his claim to the first place in Europe. And since all new treaties are based upon the precedent of old ones, and probably refer to measures taken under previous treaties, they are always drawn up in the same form, and often in the same number of articles. Now in drawing up a treaty it is the duty of the enlightened diplomat to see that the statement of policy contained in the document in hand does not conflict with or injure some other enterprise of his government. He must also see that the conditions are laid down so clearly that they cannot be subject to diverse interpretations. It is obvious from this that the negotiator must be master of the language in which the negotiation is conducted, and especially that in which the treaty itself is written, otherwise he will find himself in endless difficulties and complications. The meaning of a treaty may easily turn on a single word, and unless the diplomatist is thoroughly at home in the language in question he will not be in a position to judge whether the words proposed to be used are suitable.

ON THE MANNER OF

Ignorance of foreign languages indeed is perhaps the most serious drawback with which diplomacy can be afflicted. Now though princes and sovereign states entrust negotiations to diplomatists armed with full powers, none the less they never conclude or sign treaties except upon their own explicit ratification given with their own hand and sealed with their own seal, and the treaties are never published until they have been ratified, and cannot take effect until they are published except in cases specially provided for, where certain articles and sometimes the whole treaty is deliberately kept secret.

On Writing Despatches. While the art of handling a foreign court is the principal part of diplomacy, it is no less important that the diplomatist himself should be able to give an exact and faithful account in writing of his own court, both in respect of the negotiations in his charge and in respect of all other business which arises. The letters which a diplomatist writes to his prince are called despatches, and should be stripped of verbiage, preambles, and other vain and useless ornaments. They should give a complete account of his actions, beginning with his first *démarche* on arrival at the foreign court, describing in detail the manner in which he was received, and thereafter proceeding to report step by step the ways in which he proposes to arrive at an understanding of all that goes on around him. Thus

136

the despatches of a really adept diplomatist will present a picture of the foreign country, in which he will describe not only the course of the negotiations which he himself conducts, but a great variety of other matters which form the essential background and setting of his political action.

It will contain the portraits not only of the King *A Portrait* himself but of all his ministers, and indeed of all *Gallery.* those persons who have influence upon the course of public affairs. Thus the able diplomatist can place his master in command of all the material necessary for a true judgment of the foreign country, and the more successfully he carries out this part of his duties, the more surely will he make his master feel as though he himself had lived abroad and watched the scenes which are described. In present circumstances all French diplomatists, both ambassadors and envoys, are permitted the honour of communicating direct with the King in order to give account of their stewardship abroad, whereas in previous times they were only allowed to transmit their reports through a Secretary of State for Foreign Affairs. The latter procedure undoubtedly caused them to be more circumspect both in the matter and in the style of their despatches. This is to be regretted, for there is nothing more important than that the diplomatist living abroad should feel himself able to write with candour, freedom, and force, in all his efforts to describe the land in which he lives.

Qualities of a Good Despatch. The best despatches are those written in a clear and concise manner, unadorned by useless epithets, or by anything which may becloud the clarity of the argument. Simplicity is the first essential, and diplomatists should take the greatest care to avoid all affectations such as a pretence of wit or the learned overweight of scientific disquisitions. Facts and events should be set down in their true order, and in such a manner as to enable the proper deductions to be made from them. They should be placed in their right setting to indicate both the circumstances and the motives which guide the action of foreign courts. Indeed, a despatch which merely recites facts, without discussing them in the light of the motives and policy of persons in authority, is nothing more than an empty court chronicle. The right kind of despatch need not be long, for even the fullest discussion of motive and circumstance can be presented in a compact form; and the more compact and clear it is, the more certainly will it carry conviction to the reader.

On Keeping a Diary. This leads me to suggest that the diplomatist will find it useful to make a daily note of the principal points of which he must render an account, and he should make a special practice of sitting down at his desk immediately he comes from a royal audience, and writing out to the best of his recollection exactly what was said, how it was said, and how it was received. This diary, which is a valuable part of diplomatic equipment, will greatly assist him in composing his despatches, and will give him a means of correcting his own memory at any later date. He should draw up his despatches in the form of separate short articles, each to a single special point, for if he were to present his despatch in one unwieldy, unbroken paragraph it might never be read. A shrewd old negotiator of my acquaintance said with truth that a despatch written in an orderly fashion and in several short clear paragraphs was like a palace lighted by many windows so that there was not a dark corner in it.

Besides his diary, the negotiator should keep an *Orderly Archives.* exact minute of all the despatches which he writes, and should preserve them in chronological order for easy reference. He should do the same with those which he receives. . A properly organised registry is a good thing for the negotiator. There are certain negotiators who on sitting at their desks at night write down everything which they have learnt or guessed during the day, so that they may always be ready to supply from this journal the raw material, so to speak, of their judgments of events. It is sometimes wise to follow the practice of the Roman Court, and to devote separate letters, separately sealed, to each of the principal subjects on which despatches are being sent. This is especially the case where it is necessary to supply an ambassador with instructions upon several different points, for he may be required to produce his instructions to the Foreign Minister, and it would be well that he should be able to do so regarding points at issue without revealing the instructions he has received on other subjects.

When important negotiations are on hand no expense should be spared in keeping an efficient service of couriers, though on the other hand the young diplomatist should beware of sending anything by special courier which is not of the very first importance. . . .

Discretion in Despatch Writing. It is for the negotiator himself to make up his mind how freely he may write regarding the persons and events of a foreign country. It would be wise for him to make up his mind to the extent to which he can rely on the good faith either of his own King or of his Foreign Minister, for it is conceivable that the despatches which he writes may be shown to the prince or the ministers described in them. In this, as in many other matters, the diplomatist must know the characters both of the personage whom he describes and of the personages to whom his despatches are addressed. As he sits at his desk composing his despatch he should remember

how important a link he is between two great
nations ; how much may turn upon the manner in
which he presents his reading of events to his own
government, and therefore how vital and far-
reaching are the interests confided to his hands.
Remembering this he will instruct his secretary
and the attachés of his embassy to act as the eyes
and ears of his diplomacy, and to imitate his example
by keeping a careful daily record of impressions,
events, and persons. By comparing notes with his
subordinates he will be able all the better to carry
out one of his principal duties, which is to distinguish with care between doubtful and true
information.

It often happens that news is most uncertain at *News in its*
the moment when it is most important. He should *Proper Setting.*
therefore take care to transmit it in the proper
setting of all its attendant circumstances, so that
the prince may have some material by which to
judge whether the advice of his ambassador is well
founded. There is no doubt that in crises of this
kind the habit of private correspondence between
the Foreign Minister and the King and his ministers
abroad is of the utmost use, for it enables them to
discuss all questions with a freedom which is denied
to despatches of a more formal kind ; and it will
often place the home government in possession of
knowledge which will be of the utmost value to

them. And since a true judgment of events in one country will often depend upon what is happening in others, a diplomatist in foreign parts will ever keep in touch with his colleagues in other foreign countries, so that he may be informed of the course of events elsewhere. This co-operation between ambassadors abroad is one of the most useful features in diplomacy.

Ciphers.   As secrecy is the very soul of diplomacy, the art of writing letters in cipher has been invented in order to disguise the written message, but unless the cipher is unusually clever the industry of men, whose wits are sharpened by necessity and by self-interest, will not fail to discover the key to it. Indeed, to such a pitch has this been brought that there are now men who are known as professional decipherers, though in all probability, as I believe, their reputation rests largely upon the ineptitude of poor ciphers rather than upon their discovery of a good cipher. For as a matter of fact experience shows that a well-made and well-guarded cipher is practically undiscoverable except by some betrayal, that is to say, that the wits even of the cleverest student of ciphers will fail to pierce its secret unless aided by corruption. It is therefore the duty of the ambassador, having satisfied himself that the ciphers of his government are adroitly made, to take all means for their due protection, and especially to satisfy himself that the staff of his embassy understand not only the use of the cipher itself, but the extreme importance of guarding it from unauthorised eyes. And certainly the ambassador ought not to adopt the indolent practice, of which I have known one or two cases, where the less important part of a despatch was written *en clair*, and the ambassador himself added the vital part in cipher. Action of that kind is a masterpiece of futility, for it leads directly to the compromise of the cipher itself. For if the letter fall into enemy hands it will not be difficult for a clever spy to divine the manner of the sentence in cipher from the context written *en clair*.

In a word, the ambassador and his staff should guard a cipher as they would the inmost secrets of their own hearts. A really effective cipher is literally worth far more than its weight in gold.

It is the duty of ministers residing at foreign *General* courts to take steps to see that nothing is there *Duties.* published contrary to the honour or reputation of their sovereign, and to take all measures necessary to prevent the circulation of stories and rumours prejudicial to his interests. The ambassador must take care to protect the interests of all his master's subjects, both in such matters as the free exercise of their religion, in which he should even offer his embassy as an asylum for those who are persecuted, and in other matters, acting as a mediator between his fellow-countrymen on occasions of dispute. At need he should be ready to assist them and in all ways to live among them on terms of easy yet dignified friendship. And, on the other hand, persons of position on visiting a foreign country should never neglect to pay their respects to their own ambassador, and it is also the ambassador's duty to remind them of their duty towards the foreign court itself. If they are persons of court standing, they will be guilty of a gross breach of etiquette unless they take the proper steps to make themselves known to the sovereign. And on all kinds of public festivity he should make it his especial care to see that the members of his own national colony take their proper share in them and are accorded their due rights. The better his relations are with his countrymen living abroad, the more surely will he discover how large are the reciprocal benefits to be gained thus, for it will often happen that unofficial persons receive information as it were by accident which may be of the utmost importance to the ambassador in his negotiations. Unless good relations exist between him and them he may remain in ignorance of important facts.

In the foregoing observations I have done no

NEGOTIATING WITH PRINCES

more than give a sketch of the qualities and duties *These Precepts* of the diplomatist. Of necessity there is much that *the Fruit of Experience.* is lacking in these fugitive notes ; but I think I may claim that all diplomatists of experience will approve of the advice I have given, and will declare that the more my precepts are observed in the practice of diplomacy, the more surely will success attend the policy of our nation. If I have laid stress upon the essentials rather than upon the form and circumstance of diplomatic work, if I have also spoken with candour, both regarding the duties of the minister at home and of his agents in foreign parts, it is because I believe that a knowledge of the truth is the necessary forerunner of fruitful reform.

My final word to diplomatists, young and old, *Diplomacy* is that in normal times they may reasonably expect *Rich in Opportunity.* that where they have given proof of sterling merit in negotiation, their services will be recognised and honours conferred upon them, and in such matters the higher honour is undoubtedly to find oneself entrusted with ever more important affairs of state. But if the diplomatist should lack such recognition, he may find his own recompense in the satisfaction of having faithfully and efficiently discharged the duties laid upon him. It has often been said that the public service is an ungrateful task in which a man must find his chief recompense within himself. If I am held to agree to this, I cannot allow it to be used as a discouragement to young men of good birth and ability from entering my own profession. Disappointment awaits us in all walks of life, but in no profession are disappointments so amply outweighed by rich opportunities as in the practice of diplomacy.